Dedication

After giving honor to Allah (swt) I dedicate this book to:

My Son
For the beauty your being has brought into my life. From the first moment I gazed into your eyes, I had nothing but undying love and affection for you. I am proud of the man you have become. You are loved, unconditionally.

My Husband
For loving and accepting me for me from the moment we met. Your undying love, affection, friendship, and support has and continues to inspire and fulfill me. You are my one true love.

My Big Brother
For your love and support even when you had no idea what I was doing or where I was going. You were always that constant in my life, my protector and my forever best friend. Your strength and determination fueled me to be the best I could be and for that, I am forever grateful.

My Little Brother
For being you, for not fitting into the mold but being your authentic self. For loving and giving all of you freely, unselfishly to those in need. For being my rock and my ear.

Table Of Contents

Acknowledgments

"The essence of greatness is the perception that virtue is enough." ~ Ralph Waldo Emerson

This project was born out of love and was divinely guided. I extend my heartfelt appreciation and gratitude to Ice from Philly, a legend in his own right, for his unwavering support and guidance. From our first conversation to our current ones, he has always been humble, honest, real, and one to never sugar coat anything. For imparting your knowledge and wisdom about the history of people, the artistry, and the culture of roller skating, I honor you. For always being available, even when your life was in disarray, I am forever grateful. For loving the preservation of culture so much and continuing to cross broken lines, acknowledging that no minor disagreement is worth cloaking our history. Ice, may you forever be given the highest honors for your talents and contributions to this culture from those in our tribe. My brother, I bid you peace and blessings.

Special praise to each person that was courageous and gracious enough to share their story. Also, for trusting that I would represent them and the culture with pride and respect, for this, I am forever grateful and indebted.

To the tribe of phenomenal skaters, DJs, skate organizers, videographers, critics, rink owners, and all those who make our ride inside and outside the rink enjoyable, know you are all appreciated more than you could ever imagine. While you may not verbally be graced with our thanks, we understand that your dedication to the skate culture is born out of love. For the richness received is not that of money, but the satisfaction of the smiles on each skater's face as they roll.

Special acknowledgments to Linwood Neverson of Sk8Kingz, Doug Mike of Sk8Vidzz, Chad Ha of SkateLyfe TV, and Tyrone Dennis for your video contributions to this project. And to many others, who may have contributed and are nameless, I thank you and send prayers and gratitude to you all.

To Mr. Bill Butler, a king of our tribe who has been a pinnacle of the African American skate culture; for his dedication to the art and preservation of its history and being a constant guide and inspiration to many. To Ms. Edna Davoll, the queen of the rink, an influence for many lady skaters; her talent, love, and tenacity to this sport are awe-inspiring. To Mr. Richard Humphrey, who not only documented his moves, but to this very day is teaching and inspiring so many skaters.

And to the many other tribe members, who push this culture forward: Donald "DJ Slydz" Candler, MsssKamille, Kenneth "Rollo" Davis, DJ Kenzo Kane, DJ Big Bert Lopez, Edward "Oneofakind" Reese, DJ Joe Bowen, Terrell Ferguson, Bryant "Bee One" Anthony, Darnell D-Nell Reckless, David "The Godfather of Skate" Miles, Mz DJ Tone, Tanya "Skaterobics" Dean, Jerry Anderson, CeCe Altius, DJ Big Bob, DJ Arson, Reggie Guns, T-Stackxz, Tyrone Dixson, Beto Lopez, Bruce Clark, Josh "Bat Smoke" Smith, DJ Christopher Paul Morales, Mahaujah Turner, Terry Davis, DJ Jay the Great, Steve Love, Tony Zane, Saletta Coleman-Pierce, Desi "Skategroove" Crawl, Genese Dean, Derrick Sutton, D Jay Soulnificient, Kevin Williams, Wes Jiggs, KappaChris Robinson, Damien "Dame-o" Hodges, DJ Tootz, Wanda Brown, Master Jay, Joanne Fontaine, Jay Beewitz, Melissa Hans, OoSo MoBetta, Roger G, Natasha "Skatebeast" Thurman, Chuck Abs, Chaz "DJ Lady P" Cunningham, Patricia "Sweet P" Bush-Ross, Phelicia Wright, Adizzle Roxanne, Chad Hicks, D-Nice, Pamela Rena, Odis Rowlett, Kelvin Holtzclaw, Kyle "Push" Dutcher, Ron "Iamskate" Caesar, Nikki Garland, Tina "2 Wheels" Barbette, Sydney Blaylock, Jerry Beck, Tiffany Mason, Jessica "Skataholic" Smith, Tempest Hall, and the list could go on forever.

So, forgive me for those not mentioned. Charge it to my mind and not my heart, check for your name in Volume II ~ Peace and Blessings.

Preface

"Out of every adversity, comes opportunity." ~ Benjamin Franklin

I find this quote to be poignant at this very moment. When COVID-19 hit, many of us had to pivot in our daily work and social lives. The impact of the virus went far and wide. It restructured life far more than any of us ever imagined or expected it would or could. Most of us have been exposed and touched on a personal level by this pandemic, whether it be via a co-worker, friend, or family member; we have all been affected in one way or another. Death came early to some, unemployment to others, loneliness to many, but vision was granted to those who sat in their silence and knew that they needed a plan.

Just as the quote states, out of every adversity, comes opportunity. The pandemic forced me, along with many others, to be still, to sit, focus, and recalibrate our lives. It was a moment where we had to accept that we were not in control. As we sat in silence, many of us began to grow and look at life, work, and personal connections in a different light. This was a moment to choose whether you would sink or swim. Many, financially impacted, were already on the verge of disaster, but as the pandemic pushed them to the limits, it was hard felt. Those ill or feeble were challenged by their health, a battle many lost. Among those who survived, however, many still had lingering health issues.

There were also those of us who were challenged on the mental front. We were in a battle of how we could be victorious and not allow our minds to be stifled.

What does victory look like to me versus what it looked like to others? I love history and the arts. I began to search my soul on what I could do versus what I was unable to do. I began to reach out to people in the skate world, to check on how they were able to continue to enjoy this "hobby" as some call it. As the roller rinks closed and many states went into lockdown, skaters began to roll in their kitchens, garages, on boardwalks, tennis courts, sidewalks, and rooftops, but we skated, nonetheless.

This was our outlet, our retreat from this state of deprivation, from dealing with the not-so-pretty issues that faced us. Roll and release. Once the music comes on, and those wheels hit the ground, all the worries go into the air. You become one with the universe within those thirty, forty, or sixty minutes of freedom. Nothing else matters but your movement in the wind, on the concrete, wood, or whatever surface you could find to roll on. We have freedom, if only for just a short while. Our minds are free. Our bodies are free. We are in our zone and the world is beautiful.

That is the euphoric feeling I had when I decided to embark on this journey to present our stories, our truths, and our feelings about what the art and culture of skating means to us, in our own words.

Note that each story is written by the skaters themselves. It is their experience, their journey on how they met and fell in love with this little thing called roller skating. I pray that I have brought to life and honored their story as well as their journey in hopes that it may educate, encourage, and enlighten each reader so that they may get to know, love, and ultimately decide to connect and join us on this journey. This was the opportunity born out of this tragedy.

From The Streets, To The Stage, To The Silver Screen

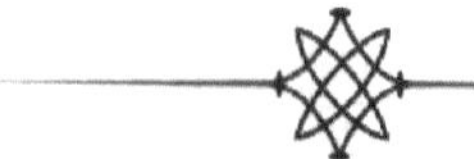

Clyde McCoy aka Ice from Philly

I have been roller skating since the age of two. Starting in Philadelphia, PA, at the Saint Charles Borromeo skating rink, my passion began at this age, when my brother (Robert Horsey, the house DJ) took me to the rink. My mother and brother were also skaters. Over the years, I began honing my skills at several rinks across Philadelphia, in the Tri-state area, and across the United States.

During this time, I incorporated several dance disciplines including Tap dance, Breakdance, Ballet, Jazz, Modern, Stepping/Hoofing along with Martial Arts. I was a member of the Franchise Dancers. I, along with several other dancers watched and stole moves from The Nicolas Brothers, The Berry Brothers, Fred Astaire, Gene Kelly, Soul Train Dancers, and many other dancers worldwide. While watching, myself and fellow skaters attempted these moves while on roller skates.

Between 1981-1982, I came across a group of guys, the Philadelphia Wizards on Wheels, who came in the rink a half hour before closing and shut it down, performing for at least 15 minutes.

From 1982-1985, The Wizards disbanded due to life events. In 1986-87, I was skating with my partner at the time, Lisa Campolo. We formed the duo High Energy. It was during this time, I asked other top skaters in Philly to join us. We also recruited two original founding members of the Wizards. During a subsequent meeting, Lisa and I embraced the name change to The Wizards on Wheels.

From 1987-2005, The Wizards was a household name in Philly, performing at all of the city's major events including parades, cultural events, and music venues. We also performed in movies and on tours with notables such as Kirk Franklin, Tom Joyner, Public Enemy, and many others.

I have been a professional roller skating artist for over 30 plus years, alongside several Philadelphia-based roller skating performing groups including Rhythm on Wheels (1984-1986) and High Energy (1986-1987). I assisted with performances by Wheels of Fire (1992-1994), acted as the frontman with The Philadelphia Wizards on Wheels (1987-2014), worked with several dance companies, and performed as a Solo Artist from 2008 to the present in over 9 different countries.

I have been a member of SGA/AFTRA since 1987 and have appeared in several Motion Pictures (including Luther's Choice, The Rocky Series, Philadelphia, The Special Feature section of Roll Bounce, Law Abiding Citizen, and Creed I and II) as an extra. I have also been featured in several magazines, newspapers, and TV commercials. In addition, I have performed at several world-famous venues in the United States including The Apollo, The Uptown, The Grand Old Opry, The Lincoln Center, Valley Forge Music Fair, Central Park, Venice Beach Skate Park, The Residence Rink and have performed for Mayors and Presidents, including a performance at President Obama's Inauguration. I have also performed with several celebrities, actors, musicians, and Broadway performers. One of my major highlights in skating is when I taught an autistic child how to skate and working with the Special Olympics.

I have helped many of my fellow roller skating artists over the years within the skating community and continue to seek wisdom and guidance from my elders worldwide.

Depths of Skating

L. David Stewart aka NIZM

My name is L. David Stewart. To those in the community of skating (rhythm), I am known as NIZM (nye-zim). I identify as a JB skater but have grown versed in other styles such as Snap and Fast backward. I hail from Chicago and am a member of a brotherhood/menagerie of personalities known as Suicide Kings.

The evolution of skating has been predicated on the following from my perspective:

The music

The internet

The history

For the reader, I speak from the vantage point of a skater who has been skating for thirty-two years at the time this was written. I have been a JB skater for twenty-two of those years. Also, I have been blessed to travel throughout the United States to observe and participate in various events of skating. I have also grown to become a fan of the culture and various skaters.

The Music

One of the most important elements of skating is music. If you disagree, skate with no music and you will intuitively think of a song to syncopate your movement too. Music and skating are synonymous; yet, enough has not been covered on the importance of music. As a JB skater, many associate the style with the late artist James Brown and his music from the timeframe of his second band in the 1970s. There is some truth in that; however, there are other artists such as Phil Collins and Led Zepplin whose music are almost canonical to JB music. JB music in its classical form is about rhythm, groove, and synchronized moves to the music. This is almost like gliding, similar to the definition listed above in skating.

A critical moment for JB skating was around 2002, when the remixes began. The remixes, anchored by a producer named Keezo Kane, began sampling James Brown music and creating new soundscapes with hip hop drum patterns to reinvigorate and reintroduce "The JBs" to a new generation. From this, spawned a new type of music, not only in Chicago, but in the international skate scene.

Today, with many producers and contemporary music, as the music has morphed, so has JB skating. Without belaboring the point, to understand the transition of the music, one only needs to attend an "ole school session" versus a "new school session" to see the difference in not only the music, but also in the tempo, age range, and vibe. This phenomenon is not exclusive to JB but recognized across the United States. As people come and go from their respective skate scenes, new generations improve and alter that which was before them. Music is a driving force in that change.

The Internet

Here is a tool that has reshaped our view and how we do everything. Someone may be reading this chapter on a device that was unfathomable 20 years ago.

When I started skating in the late summer of 1989, cell phones were not a part of everyday life. To learn about skating, you had to go to the skating rink. There was no way to experience skating in any capacity unless you were present. The internet and apps such as Facebook, Instagram, and TikTok now allow people to see what skaters do. This has been a double-edged sword.

On one hand, it shows the craft that many of us have been passionate about, and on the other hand, it has contributed to the reduction of skating rinks. Also, it is making people feel like experts on a culture they haven't experienced for themselves in person just because they watched a few YouTube videos. That dichotomy goes hand-in-hand with evolution, nonetheless.

Without the internet, many skaters would not have been discovered, opportunities wouldn't be had, and friendships wouldn't have been forged. This would have made us miss other positive characteristics that have made skating popular.

The internet has also allowed skating to be utilized as a revenue generator because skaters are now appearing on shows (example: The Chi), as well as commercials, and other tools for advertising products and services.

Businesses and brands are now seeking out skaters because it has become trendy to utilize skaters in promotion. This was further exacerbated by TikTok during this pandemic, presenting a pseudo-revival of skating. Pseudo revival, in this case, because skating never went away for many across the country, bringing me to the last element.

The History

Without a full rehash, skating has its own roots that vary in different communities. In the case of African Americans, there have been cultural and historical implications over the 20th century, where skating wasn't just "an escape" but a means of protest and fighting for identity and equality. For more on this, please view the documentary, "United Skates Documentary."

Each style has a history of creation and growth that has explicitly contributed to the evolution of skating overall. If a style has a home, it has a history, creators, originators, and innovators. Often, those individuals are not found unless you go to that particular style's birthplace to meet individuals, who may not travel but are passionate about this thing we call skating.

History is fluid and, in the present, we are contributing to a future that will be tomorrow's past. So, today's innovation is tomorrow's classic. Hundreds and thousands of skaters comprise this history and each has a history full of dynamism, which makes it what it is, each as unique as a raindrop. And that is what makes skating so powerful.

As skating continues to grow, it is important to document not just the big names, but the small people as well as big and small events. To have a broad swath of understanding, the historian must write from the perspective of the unknown as opposed to the popular. Similar to when a skater is just learning by studying the expert and the beginner. Lessons can be found in both. The evolution of skating as it goes forward will be through the music, the internet, and the history that is yet to be created.

The Birth Of Skate Love Barcelona

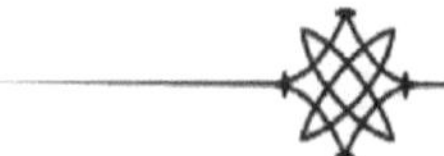

Michelle Barrios

"Love is in the air ... The beach, the sun, the smooth surface, the breeze, the excitement, the community, the love ... Just the most fabulous, friendly, welcoming, inclusive festival in the world."

"Every skater needs to visit this festival at least once. Beware though, once you've been to this festival, you won't want to leave. And I guarantee you'll be back, sharing the skate love every year after." - Sk ☰ **Julie - Skatefit Edinburgh**

"Definitely one the best skate party experiences! Skating on a beautiful beach with beautiful people, you can't go wrong!"- **Sheila Gray Houston**

"The best spot in the world for lovers of eight wheels and good music. A world of smiles and love in your eyes." - **Romuald CHAPELET La Rotonde (Geneva - CH)**

"Roller skating itself has its merits anyhow. But rolling at the beachfront with the best from places all over the world, in a city that has an ancient history, yet has so many modern, progressive people, it's awesome. Don't take it away from me, it's my personal skating X-mas." - **Leslie Phunkster**

"It was great. Dancing with people from everywhere in harmony. Just having fun ☰☰☰ ." - **Inge Boer**

"This was my first time and I had a total blast. Thank you so much for organizing this fantastic event. The atmosphere, disco, shows, beach party, workshops, and amazing music were all wonderful." - **Hanna Parry**

"Absolutely amazing event with gorgeous skaters from across the globe." -

The Founder's Journey.

My name is Michelle Barrios and I've been a roller skater since my childhood. I'm originally from Panama and I grew up skating at a rink called, "El Patín Dorado" (The Golden Skate). I don't have images to document my happiness from that time, but I do have my diary from when I was eleven years old, where I wrote about my happiness from skating.

Unfortunately, the rink closed. After that, my skates were stolen, and I stopped skating and focused on my other passions. Apart from my career as a Graphic Designer, I was an advertising model, dancer, hostess, and singer in Panama. I decided to experience the world. Thus, in 1999, I moved to Madrid, Spain and came back to skating. I never thought that I would come back to my childhood passion as an adult, and even more, to create something out of it.

After several visits to Barcelona and discovering the great vibes and surfaces of the city, I moved to Barcelona in 2006. One day, I found some quad skaters and we immediately connected. They had the idea of organizing an outdoor party and invited me to join the team, which I did and started to help with graphics and promotion. After the project was over, I created my own brand to spread the roller dance vibes on Facebook as BCN Roller Dance. It started as a meetup community, where we started to organize small events, to dance for private shows or films (advertising/music videos), or to give classes.

The Start of a Movement.

There wasn't a roller dance movement in Barcelona around 2010-2012, so I started to post about other communities to show how cool this is and to grab attention. Mainly showcasing the outdoor movements from Central Park, NYC, Venice Beach, and London because we didn't have an indoor rink until recently.

I was always trying to bring this culture to Barcelona, creating interesting content to get new skaters to join us. In 2012, we were visited by thirteen international skaters. That visit was the start of the International Roller Dance Jam in Barcelona that grew organically from 2012 to 2014, putting Barcelona in the spotlight of skate events.

After seeing the growth and rise in people's interest through the years, I felt it was time to make it a proper festival. I created the brand 'Skate Love Barcelona' in 2015. At that time, the festival promotions were part of BCN Roller Dance channels, but in 2018, I started to promote the festival on its own channels.

Starting 'Skate Love Barcelona' was extremely difficult. We started the festival with no infrastructure, money, or experience in this type of event to hold such a program. We didn't understand many things. We didn't have a "roller disco" culture here and special venues that can be used to roller skate weren't all that helpful. As if this were not enough, some people who didn't understand or trust my vision, decided to make things even more complicated by trying to sabotage the event.

Fortunately, the result of the first edition of 'Skate Love Barcelona' in 2015 was so magical that everyone was excited about the experience. It was a successful beginning and an emotional experience. The first edition of the festival was key to knowing and understanding what exactly we had. It helped us realize that there was a very open community willing to be part of our proposal.

The support received in the first edition surprised us. We did not have funds to cover the costs of our collaborators, but we were fortunate to have the support of many. Among them were the coaches, who came all the way from Australia to teach and share with the participants, to spread the love. One of the richest aspects of this event is the multicultural and intergenerational exchange.

From day one, strong ties were created, thanks to the affection of many collaborators. They bet on the festival with us, and likewise, we received honest feedback. This helped us perceive how our festival made a positive impact in many lives. My motivation is fueled by the amount of support that we have received throughout the four years of the festival, especially from those who contributed to the first edition offering their time, energy, talent, passion, and love to make it happen.

The Definition and New Goals
'Skate Love Barcelona' is an international music festival on skates, dedicated to a community that shares the passion for music, dancing, and

rolling in a social and multicultural environment. Our mission is to grow and inspire the community, keeping the essence of our common passion with respect, love, and solidarity regardless of cultures, races, and genders. We want to help transform our world by delivering a distinctive festival while taking action to meet the SDGs - Sustainable Development Goals. Thus, we are very excited about this new commitment.

We are proud to currently meet several of these goals. According to the SDG's website, "The Sustainable Development Goals are the blueprint to achieve a better and more sustainable future for all. They address the global challenges we face, including poverty, inequality, climate change, environmental degradation, peace, and justice."

Skate Love Barcelona is a four day event that happens in eight locations, being the biggest and most expensive production that includes indoor Skate Love Disco and an outdoor Beach Party. Both parties have to be created from scratch in empty spaces, putting the electricity, the lighting, bar, DJ table, and counting on the permission for the boardwalk closure.

We have a great program of eight indoor and outdoor activities. The activities include workshops in three different settings, the Barcelona city tour, Meet & Greet with the Biz, Networking for the skaters that want to promote their businesses, the Skate Love Disco, the Beach Party, and the Gastronomic Closure. And for this year's edition, we are working on introducing a new and exciting surprise activity. The workshops have been a crucial area of our festival due to the number of people interested in learning and improving their skills with great coaches from all over the world.

Skate Love has been growing organically year by year, and we keep doing our best to offer an amazing experience for the community. In 2021, we will be celebrating our fifth anniversary, seeing that we have already noticed a bigger interest than last year's event. Consequently, we are expecting around twelve hundred people from thirty countries at this year's edition.

Stay True to Your Dreams

Nine years ago, I started my skating projects with the mere intention of creating a local community where I can enjoy my passion for skating. I never imagined that it would become what it is today. Time puts everything in its place. If you keep the hard work, perseverance, and passion; if you take care of your project's essence and values, if you keep your eyes open to learning from your mistakes with humility, and most importantly if you keep the mental balance while working on your project, you can achieve amazing things.

From Mr. JB to Mr. IR

Darius Stroud aka D-Breez

I am fortunate that skating was generational in my family; both my mother and father skated. My sister also skated. My nieces and nephews skate as well. My father had trophies lined up against the wall from his participation in skating contests and was a competitive skater. My mother was a smooth jazzy skater. Skating is something I was born with. I wish others could understand that having a competitive nature is a good thing. It propels us to be better. The people I competed with helped me to become as good as I was. They constantly pushed me to be better so that I could receive the smiles and applause in the rink.

At our local rink, some great skaters were legendary, and they used to meet up in the middle or as we say, "crazy legging in the middle."

When I came up, there would be a group of legends including Poochie, Milt, Nate, and others. These guys were legendary, and they welcomed everyone. They never gave other skaters the stank face, shunned anyone, or came out to obliterate one's move when one came in the middle. Rather, they would applaud, correct, and encourage others, even showing them a move or two.

Back in the day, when I used to see skaters trying to do my moves, if we were cool, I would assist them on how to get the move correct. This was one of the remarkable things about skating with the older generation (OG's). But there is also the other side to that gentleness, there will be people who don't like you. Either way, it works out for the good.

My rivals would push and inspire me, so I couldn't stop being creative with my moves. As they learned my moves, I knew I had to come out with other moves to stay on top. All rivals became fuel for my fire.

A fun fact about me: I'm a gamer. My main game of choice is Grand Theft Auto 5. For the last seven to eight years, it has been unbelievable. My other games are NBA2K basketball, Call of Duty War Zone, Gran Turismo racing, and Assassin's Creed. There are a lot of skaters that are Gamers.

Gaming is another way to stay connected. The gaming world was our first experience with social distancing. It's a way for people from all over the world to connect without being physically together. The competitiveness in some of the games, for me, is equivalent to skating.

A humble understanding comes with growing older. With age, you begin to reflect on those who assisted you to get to your current level. We all learn things from others. The difference with skating is that when you come into it, you see something intriguing and you want to learn it. You begin to learn directly from someone you know and tend to skate like them. A learner tries to mimic the teacher, but one must learn the move and add creativity to the move.

The Chicago based, JB style, which is a beautiful style, is now the dominating style nationwide. You must learn the foundation of the style whenever you want to start using it. Then, as you advance, you will begin to put your own creative twist on it.

I would be a bad instructor, because I am the type of person that would have a hard time teaching you from the beginning if you want to learn a skate move. I lack the patience. Nonetheless, when you get your balance or reach a certain level, I can help you to understand what you are missing and guide you to perfect the move. I didn't learn directly from a lot of people. My personal style of learning is to watch a person and then apply my own creativity to it. There were a few people throughout the years that I did ask directly. I watched others and applied their methods as well.

This method allowed my mind to see their moves, break it down, and then figure out how it works with my body. I advise newcomers to try this method of learning.

The Nutcracker, a signature move that I was known for, made a lot of people think I studied this move and perfected it, but that's not how it happened. People from my old neighborhood and school knew that I used to dance. I liked Break Dancing, Michael Jackson, James Brown, MC Hammer, and the likes. Through dancing, I was able to do the splits. While dancing, someone would always challenge or battle me. At one dance event, someone challenged me, and I wanted to win. I decided I would drop into a split and come up immediately. I did just that. With the adrenaline pumping in my veins, I knew I had nailed it. It was like I won the Championship.

I brought the move to skating. I had seen someone in the Michael Jackson video do this move on skates. When my guys challenged me, I thought, "What the hell! I'm going to try this move."

I had never attempted this move on skates in the past, but like clockwork, I dropped it and pulled it back up with the shoulder wave. It was crazy. The crowd went wild. It goes back to my competitive nature, and I knew I nailed it yet again.

Then, on another date, a DJ mentioned how they used to jump five feet in the air and land in the splits. So, I pictured it in my mind, did that too, and nailed it.

Regarding being a GOAT (Greatest of All Times), of skating, can anyone ever master all the skate styles? I don't think so. No one is going to be great in every area. It's not about being a master of all styles but mastering yours. If you are on a stage with other masters of their own style, who's going to shine the brightest? That's when you become a GOAT. I've witnessed people, whom you know are good, shy away from a contest. Some feel the spotlight is too bright and that's not what they are made for. Off the stage, that person is amazing, but on the stage, they crack under the pressure, whereas someone else can perform under pressure.

A GOAT is not the best skater of the year. They are the best skater of an Era. You have to put in a body of work as a great skater in your area. When you are that good as a skater, you change the atmosphere around you. When others want to skate like that person and learn from that person, that is the GOAT.

Skating is a hobby that we all do and enjoy. But as a GOAT, you're able to do something that people with boatloads of money, with powerful jobs cannot always do; something that they, in some instances, may never be able to do. You are creating something that can impact their lives and create a change within people. I also give accolades to people when their props are due. Even back in the day, I did this. It's humbled respect. You have to respect a craft you love before you can be great. You must be able to see greatness and appreciate greatness in others.

When you accomplish something that you set out to do, there is a euphoric moment. But what comes after that? Now that you have achieved being the best in your rink, what's next? Now, you must experience a few losses to appreciate your accomplishments. You must also understand what accomplishment is. When people congratulate you on a win, how do you respond? People want to be great, but don't know what comes with that. When you are labeled 'great', half of the skate world will love you and half of them will hate you, can you handle that? Then, you will try and remain that guy/girl for five, ten, or twenty years. It's lonely at the top, especially if you are not a people person.

For you to accomplish anything and remain on top, you must have people around you that can remind you why you are doing this. If no one congratulates you, what does it mean? The difference between the people on top and those who stay at the top is like those who are one-hit wonders in the music world.

When you are the champ or on top, you are elated. You have people coming at you from different directions for all the wrong reasons. You have no guidance because it's new and now you have to do something on this level or better to remain relevant. Those people tend to break under the pressure, they drug out, fall out, or they quit because most don't surround themselves with people who will challenge them, and tell them when they are wrong. If you are doing it for yourself, you must have some type of self-gratification that allows you to say, 'I'm cool'; otherwise, you end up being the best skater but you're hollow inside.

What you thought the win would fill within, you never get. You feel empty and lonely despite being the best. Now, you're looking at everyone else and feeling you have no meaning. It's like not being human because you have no emotion. That is the result of being lonely at the top and not knowing what to do next.

One thing I love and have always loved about skating is that you can do it alone and you can do it everywhere. You can also excel and be a star in your own right. My whole JB elite skate team were skaters who showed a higher level of skating. I had to respect not only their level of skating but their differences. People always seem to think a skate group must skate alike. Not my group. As good as I was, my friend, Tito, would have destroyed me in a crazy leg circle, and I knew it. When there would be a challenge in the middle, I would send Tito in the middle to destroy them. As a leader, I was able to identify and respect each of our team member's strengths and weaknesses.

Once national skate parties started to take off, Tito and I started to travel the country, not to lay down the law, but to experience the world with this skating stuff. You should travel the world so that you can appreciate your city. You can skate and do what you love to do everywhere now.

When we travel, the driver gets to choose the music. When I drive, many would assume my music of choice would be rap or hip hop, but I listen to a wide range of music. Most of the songs I listen to are aggressive like DMX's "What's My Name", or club bangers like Lil Jon & Bone Crusher's "I Ain't Never Scared", or strong thought-provoking like TI's "Still I stand", or pain-filled like Bon Jovi's "Wanted", and more. A lot of the music I listen to puts you in the mood or mindset to conquer something or to meet a challenge. I can also flip it to laid back music like Rick Ross' "Aston Martin Music." I love "In the Air Tonight" by Phil Collins. You have to be diverse musically. I used to Break Dance to Herbie Hancock "Rock It". We used to throw a piece of cardboard on the ground and go to work. Music is beautiful.

These days, JB music is progressive. Back in the days, we had three tempos - real slow like "Watermelon Man", mid-tempo like "Watergate", and then the high tempo like "Make it Funky" and "Cornbread." These days, DJ's are stuck on the high tempo, I wish we could go back to at least two tempos.

The thing I love about National and International parties like Independence Roll (IR) and other current skate events are that they are multi-racial and religious, everyone is welcome. We get more appreciation to see a variety of people from all over the world, to see all the varied skate styles and cultures. Once you start to travel and begin to see the world, you begin to appreciate the differences. It really opens your eyes to life. Let skating be your excuse to travel the world. Seeing the world allows you to appreciate your style even more. Before national skate parties and my travels, I didn't know if I even wanted friends outside of Chicago, but after experiencing travel, I was open to communicating with others all over the country. When you see other people from other countries attending these events and know that you and a total stranger actually love one another because of skating, you are experiencing something beautiful.

I built Independence Roll on music that touches people around the world. I choose DJs for the event that will touch all styles and cultures. When I began to travel nationally, the only time we would get to hear our music (JB) was during roll call and we used to show out when we were called to the skate floor. While I understood it, I didn't agree with it. We (JB skaters) would only get the last five or ten minutes of the night to skate to our music, outside of the roll call. It was sad. Now, you can hear JB music everywhere. It has been an adjustment for the DJ's and skaters. Over time, people have gotten used to skating to the music. Many are not even skating the JB style to the music, which is beautiful. Now, more producers are bringing the style to the music as well.

When we put IR together and I was choosing the DJ's, DJ DMC was a no brainer. He has been on board since day one and will be with me until he wants to stop.

DJ Joe Bowen also came on board in the beginning as he began gaining listeners from other states and is still rocking with me. Then, I went to get DJ Narcissistic from Ohio because he was making great noise in his area. Moreover, I wanted to let people know that IR wasn't just a JB party, that it was a national party and we would play all styles of music. Mz DJ Tone was our first female DJ, who was making noise outside of our city, and I felt like I could help. DJ Fly Ty and I had met inside Branch Brook Park skating rink in NJ a few years earlier. I liked his approach to learning JB music.

DJ Lil Brian is like a nephew. I helped him connect with a few event coordinators when he was a youngster on the scene. DJ CJ was the next phase of our up and coming DJ talents in our style. DJ Arson drove to the first IR after spinning at an event Friday night and brought other skaters with him. I admired that.

All the DJs are people I know, who are handling music on a national level, not just a local level. I also paired them up on various nights so that they can represent everyone, making it easier to convince others of our vision. I have also created a platform for new DJs to get introduced on a national level. In the last couple of years, I have been allowing young DJs to get a feature spot, giving them exposure as it is hard for a new DJ to get exposure on a national level.

The South Got Something To Skate

Paul Johnson

It all started one Friday night at Sparkles skating rink in Riverdale. Doug, the reason I even started skating, had been asking me and my homie, Dean, whom I have known since I was nine, about skating at the rink. We fought him about it constantly and even made some bias comments about skating.

Doug wouldn't take 'no' for an answer. So, he basically put his whole allowance up to pay for anything we wanted that Friday night. All he needed was to physically show us his vision. Eventually, Dean and I went with him. We didn't even get past the DJ booth before Doug was swarmed by pretty females, greeting and hugging him. We looked at each other like, 'damn'.

We didn't even think it was honeys at the rink like that. He then took us into the Pro Shop and rented us our speed skates. They looked cool compared to the brownies or should I say rental skates. He told us to hold off on putting them on as they were playing some dance music. Afterwards, we headed to the corner to dance with some ladies before we laced up. In fact, I hadn't even spent a half-hour in the rink, and I was already sold on going again because I had ladies and popularity in the blink of an eye.

Doug said, "Get ready to skate because after the slow set, they gonna play our music."

We were like, "Wait! We have music?"

The slow set was over and 'chief rocka' started playing, and Doug started going crazy.

We were like, "Let's go."

Mind you, we couldn't do a *damn* thing but roll and try not to fall. Meanwhile, Doug was doing all types of tricks and a cross slide or known to the ATL OGS as the stab. Dean and I were sold. We were like, "We gotta learn this."

I went home and curved my schedule around Friday nights. We started practicing weekly. No week off. No month off. After about a year and a half, the manager of the rink called us to his office and told us, he would allow us to start skating on Sunday Adult night, if we didn't fight, respected our elders, and didn't cuss.

We were like, "Okay, we're in."

By this time, I was the skate guard at SkateTowne, and Dean was the DJ. So, we never had to work at our rink on Friday or Sunday nights. Instead, we practiced on Fridays at Sparkles and Saturday nights at SkateTowne while we were on the clock.

Finally, the first Sunday came and we went. It was scary and super packed. Nonetheless, we skated well. The catch was that there were like seven to ten other skate crews, with names, chants, and popularity. We were some kids from the ghetto, who weren't supposed to be there, but we held our own. We were getting waxed by the superior group (Vaughn's Crew). I had known him all these years and never knew the name of their crew. All I knew was when the blonde high-top fade was coming, you better get out of the way. There were other crews too. We made up names for them because we didn't know their names and didn't care.

We had one job: to be the best! We taunted and made fun of other crews, but also worked hard, to avoid looking like any of them. Our moves were super hard to replicate. Some of the crews didn't take kindly to us and a lot of skaters complained to management that we were too young to be there, but we were backed by management. They couldn't do anything about it.

We started getting really good and climbed the chart on our way to the top. We also went through a lot of tough times and met haters along the way. They still try to hate on DA ONES, but we reign Supreme.

I remember one night we were on our way home from the rink and stopped at a red light only to have a rival skate crew pull up on us and draw a gun on us. I stared down the barrel of a gun and didn't flinch. It's funny that years later I saw the guy who pulled a gun out on me. He said, "Hey man! We wanted to scare y'all away from the rink. I wasn't gonna shoot y'all."

I also want to give a shout out to the Gorilla Brothers, with whom we always go into the game, alongside the Jungle Brothers, my Philly strut crew (Pops, Unk, Mike, the twins, and the whole family), Courtney and Ivan's crew, Kojak and Tee, Kelvin and Jamar (The Warriors), Ga. Rampage, S.O.S, ATL squad, and last but not least, Vaughns' crew. You all pushed us to raise the bar in this ATL skate style world.

On our way to the top, we also had a special skate night with Destiny's Child. Me, Doug, Dean, and Titus were at the rink one Sunday night, when we came across a group of four beautiful women. It was a match made in heaven. Every member of the crew except Doug kept trying to match me up with Latoya Luckett, who was taller than I was. I was barely six ft tall. He was six foot three. However, I got over to this other lady, that I had eyes on from the jump and asked her if I could skate with her. She looked at me like she wasn't coming unless her girls had someone to skate with. On cue, Dean, Doug, and Titus chose one of the girls.

Dean grabbed Kelly, Doug grabbed Latoya, and Titus grabbed the chocolate girl (I never knew her name). We all got to skate with them, showed out, and got to skate with them again. When the slow set came back, it was one of the best skate sessions I had. There was no drama from rival crews and no falls. We were flawless on the routines, and each of us had a lady to skate with all night. When it was time to go, we all went over to them to exchange numbers. Here, I got one piece of paper I wish I had saved because it had my partner's phone number and name. She wrote her name on the paper. It said, "Bianca."

I said, "Okay, Bianca. I'm a call you."

She said, "That's not my name."

Then, she took the paper and wrote (BE-YON-CE). She told me they were staying at a hotel and we could come to hang out with them while they were here meeting with Jermaine Dupri and LaFace records, that they were a singing group named 'Destiny's Child'.

Later, I was trying to convince my crew that we should go hang out with them, even though we had school in the morning. We didn't go and the rest is history, they became famous. Two years later, the Limo driver saw us at the rink and proceeded to tell me that they talked about us all night and on the way back to Houston.

Years later, black people started owning skating rinks. Four were black-owned and still are today- SkateTowne, Skate Zone, Metro Fun Center, and the most famous one, Cascade, which wasn't all that popular until the movie came out.

One Sunday, we were at Cascade, and this heavyset guy with dreads came into the rink, walked around, and sat in the corner. He watched us for three hours even as we enjoyed the whole Cascade vibe. It was a nice crowd, with a few crew members, but never like Sparkles. By this time, we were the top dogs of the rink, and we are still the top dogs because if my whole group comes to the rink, you all know what time it is.

Anyway, one Tuesday, we got a call saying we needed to come up to Cascade on Wednesday morning to Shoot a commercial. We were like, "Okay!"

When we got there, we met the guy from Sunday, who said, "Y'all were killing that shit on Sunday."

And he wanted to know if he could get that same energy from us that Wednesday.

We said, "Hell yeah!"

The rest is history. Major blessings and shout outs to Chris Robinson for believing in us. He even referred us to Benny Boom for the Ciara 1'2 Step video, which was a blast from the past because we already knew Ciara from when she used to dance at Sparkles. She grew up in the same area as us, just a little younger though.

And all ATL's finest were there, 112, Killa Mike, Shawty Shawty. These were folks we knew from around the way. It made the video extra fun, clowning around with folks we grew up with. The iPod commercial was dope. We met Hi Hat (Missy Elliott's Choreographer) and she saw us skate but didn't know we could dance. We had them hyped up.

Even down to the movie, where we had to teach TI and other actors how to skate the ATL style (Meagan Good owes me a cake too…). In the twenty-eight years that Da Ones have been a group, the original three members have clocked over seven hundred fifty thousand dollars and counting. If you add DJ Slim (Brandon), it's over eight hundred thousand dollars. Who knew a seventy-five dollar pair of skates could have a return profit of two hundred fifty thousand dollars? Even though we did all these things with skating, we were still humble. I am teaching the second wave of Da Ones as we try to return to the big screen.

The quote I live by is "Skating saved my life!"

I hope it saves a lot more lives along the way. Growing up in College Park isn't a joke. So much could have happened but didn't because I was skating. Nowadays, as a skate pioneer and O.G. in the skate world, I love to educate skaters especially the new ones, who want to do the moves but don't want to pay homage. I see Facebook and Instagram posts all the time asking, "Who are the top five skaters?

I always comment, "ME."

If you are talking top five groups, 'Da Ones' is number one, hands down, and will probably be that way until I leave this earth.

<u>ABOUT THE AUTHOR:</u>
I am Paul Antonio Johnson, skate crew member of DA ONES skate crew, *repping* College Park Georgia. I am forty-three years *young*; I am the Vince Carter of roller skating. I have been a member of my skate crew since 1993. I have been relevant in the skate world for four decades.
Facebook: Paul Antonio Johnson
Instagram: @paulantoniojohnson

To view videos of the author, grab the physical copy for an interactive experience.

Birth Of The Skate Critic

Ginger Mathews aka Skate Critic

My journey began before I was born. My maternal grandmother was an ice skater. My mother was an artistic roller skater and my father was a "Rink Rat". My father would go down to Valle Vista Skating Center in Hayward, California on Friday and Saturday nights, trying to talk to my mother.

One day she told him, 'If you're trying to get me to go out with you, you're going to have to learn how to skate."

He left and told my Uncle Joe that he was done with that broad and didn't care if he ever saw her again. The following Friday, he returned with his entire paycheck and bought a pair of skates and learned how to skate. My mom passed away at twenty years old when I was only twenty-two months. She never got to take me roller skating.

My father married my second mom, who was also an artistic roller skater. She told me that I was born to skate. Later, my second mom took me skating for the first time when I was four years old. I had a lesson not long after that at Valle Vista Skating Center in Hayward, California. I was in the center of the Skate Floor, having my lesson while the Saturday afternoon session was happening around me. I was not paying attention and goofing off.

Every once in a while my second mom would come out of nowhere at skating by me at a hundred miles an hour, smacking my head and telling me to pay attention, then skate away as fast as she arrived.

All I could think was, "Wow! I want to skate fast as she does." Eventually I was able to skate faster than her.

My father passed away when I was six, so my grandparents raised me. They would drop me off at Valle Vista Skating Center every weekend. I became a Rink Rat like my father. When I was around nine or ten, I went to my Aunt's house for the summer in Roseville, California. She took me to her rink, Roller King.

I remember walking in and thinking, "What's wrong with this rink? Why is the floor blue?"

I was totally fascinated with everything different about this rink. From then on, I wanted to see inside every rink. I wanted to see what was different. My grandparents rarely obliged. When I was sixteen, I would pick up my friend Cyndi from BART (Bay Area Rapid Transportation) because she didn't drive to go to Valle Vista Skating Center.

One day she said, "You have a license and a car."

I replied, "Yeah…"

She said, "We can go to any rink we want."

I said, "YES!"

And away we went, going to other rinks, increasing my fascination.

I got married a few times, had kids, and vowed that I would not make my kids skate orphans until they could get into the adult skates. I planned all our vacations around visiting at least one rink each year. Finally, my youngest son was able to petition his way into the adult skate at San Jose Skate in San Jose, California at the age of fifteen. It was game on from there.

I come from a long line of skaters as I stated earlier. My uncle was a pro. My aunt and uncle are artistic roller skaters, roller derby, and roller hockey skaters. They also played on the Bay City Bombers and owned a rink called Roller Faire in Pleasanton, California. My family has their hands in three Roller Derby teams in the Central Valley of California, and my uncle wrote the rules for Flat Track Derby. One of my cousins was also on the Bay City Bombers, coached roller derby, played roller derby, and roller hockey. Another cousin played roller hockey and was on the USA team that won Gold. Both of their spouses are skaters too. Like I said earlier, my mom and second mom were artistic roller skaters. Grandma was an ice skater and my father was a Rink Rat. I almost forgot, my uncle/godfather was also an artistic roller skater. My grandfather worked at a traveling Roller Rink in the 1930s in Texas, and then there's me.

I went in a totally different direction from the rest of my family. I became an adult skater, following the adult circuit skate parties around the US. During my travels, I would hit as many rinks as I could. Each trip, I'd usually hit an average of ten Roller Rinks plus the skate party and a few adult skate sessions. Phew!!

My first goal was to skate at every rink in California. While accomplishing this goal, my family would often tell me, "You need to write this down. You need to take pictures. People want to know."

I would just fluff them off and say, "Yeah! Yeah! Yeah!"

Soon skaters began asking me about rinks because I had been to so many. Then, I went to a roller derby game and my Aunt said to me again, "You need to write this down. You need to take pictures. People want to know."

I said to her, "Yeah! Yeah! I'll be the 'Skate Critic'."

Lord, I had no idea what was about to happen. I completed my California goal and then a new roller rink opened in Murrieta, California. So…

I headed to the Los Angeles area on New Year's Eve 2013 to reclaim my title. I was going to the new roller rink Epic Rollertainment in Murrieta, California on New Year's Day, 2014. I thought that I would just skate at one of my other favorite roller rinks in the Los Angeles area for New Year's Eve with my friends. But no! All the LA rinks were fifteen and under lockdown, meaning that unless you had a kid with you, you weren't going! Ugh!

Here I was in my Hotel Room, bored. I thought, *let me check into this Skate Critic thing.* I searched everywhere, and no one was doing any kind of rink reviews. I went on Facebook, Instagram, Twitter, Tumbler & YouTube. I started my group "Skate Critic" with thirty-three friends in it. All night my phone would not shut up. By the next day, there were over eight hundred people in my Skate Critic group on Facebook.

When I returned from this trip and went to my local adult skate at

Golden Skate in San Ramon, California, all my friends asked me, "What did you do?"

I said, "I don't know but we're rolling with it" No Pun intended. And then, the Skate Critic was born.

Today, Skate Critic has over six thousand four hundred members. I have over ten thousand followers behind the scenes and I'm just amazed. Of course, I can't stop there.

I was absolutely annoyed with all the rink lists online. They were outdated by over seven years at that point. Today, those lists are outdated by over thirteen years. I would go to addresses listed for rinks and find empty lots. Some of them had been vacant for close to ten years. I set out to fix this problem. I downloaded every rink list and made a huge master list. Then, I proceeded to call every rink to verify that they were still in business. I hired some friends and family and we started calling. Numbers were disconnected, businesses had closed, burned down, moved, or changed area codes.

Every time, we ran into an error, we had to investigate it further to find out if the rink really was gone, the area code was changed, they changed buildings, changed names, changed owners, or if they were burnt to the ground?

After eighteen months, I had a working live rink list. It was and still is better than any list out there! Yes! No more driving to a rink to find out they were gone. The byproduct of this project was a dead rink list, which was to make sure that roller rinks are not forgotten.

As of today, my dead rink list is up to eight thousand nine hundred seventy-eight rinks in the US. I suspect there are at least two thousand more rinks I have not uncovered yet. The live rink list is one of my greatest accomplishments. I physically sit down every other year to call all of these rinks to make sure they are still in business and constantly monitor the internet to research roller rinks. My following is so massive that people notify me of rinks opening and closing all the time.

As of today, the live rink list is at one thousand two hundred forty-four rinks in the US and about seventy in the rest of the World. Many rinks have fallen during the pandemic. I will not know the extent of this damage until after it is over. Then I can sit down to physically call all the rinks to see which ones made it.

Of course, my lists don't stop there! Why should they? I have the most up to date 'For Sale Roller Rink' list in the country and a list of people looking to buy rinks. I have the most up to date 'Adult Skate Roller Rink' list, 'Adult Skate Party' list, 'Roller Rink Owners' list, 'Adult Skate Music' list, 'Black-owned Roller Rink' list, 'Future Roller Rink Owners' list, 'Master Roller Rink' list, 'Roller Rink Owners' list, 'Ages of the Rink' itself, Regular Rink Rules, Adult Skate Rink Rules, Rotunda floor list, Top Twenty-eight oldest Roller Rinks, Top Ten Largest Skate floors, Top Twenty Largest Skate floors, Top Ten Smallest Skate floors and I'm sure a few more I've forgotten.

What happens next? As I was traveling along through the skate world, reviewing Roller Rinks, I was approached at a Skate party at Roller Dome in Richmond, Virginia to be part of a skating documentary.

I said, "Sure, but you're going to have to call me because I gotta go skate."

If anyone knows me, when I'm at a Skate Party, I'm the first one on the skate floor and usually the last one off. I skate fast and hard all night. Well, they did call me for five years as we worked on this documentary. Of course, most of my work was behind the scenes checking facts. I made an appearance five times in the film with one part of a line I always say when talking about the sad fate of Our Roller Rinks in the US.

"On average, we lose three rinks a month in the US. You may get one that re-opens and maybe a new one."

There is a scene in the "United Skates Documentary" of the US Map with the locations of nearly five thousand Roller Rinks we had at one time. The clock rolls forwards and the roller rinks go away until we were left one thousand two hundred fifty-six roller rinks we had left at the end of production. This scene was all my work brought to life on the big screen. Everywhere it was shown, it brought the entire audience to tears or gasps. I cried at the premiere when I saw it and heard the audience. Finally, people were grasping what I was seeing every day.

I have reviewed and skated at three hundred ninety-eight roller rinks as of today. My current goal is to surpass Sure-Grip Steve who has visited four hundred sixty rinks. Once I achieve this goal, I can enter the Guinness Book of World records. Then, I can say I have skated at the most roller rinks in the world. Of course, I won't stop there! My other goal is to say I've skated at every roller rink in the world.

You're probably asking about my reviews. When I walk into a rink, I am looking at their floor, employees, snack bar, bathrooms, and DJ. All rinks are graded by Wheels one through eight. Example: Eight Wheels means perfect and any less than that means you have some things to work on. Eight Wheels also means you have a full set of wheels to skate on. I give out Toe Stops to rinks that are over the top after you've achieved your Eight Wheels first! To date, there are only two rinks with Eight Wheels and Two Toe Stops. Those rinks are Oaks Park Roller Rink in Portland, Oregon aka "The Oaks" and Semoran Skate Way in Casselberry, Florida.

After I am done looking for my criteria and measuring the skate floor, I then start looking at what makes this rink special from other rinks. I try to capture the uniqueness of the rink in photos and videos. When I am finished with that, I look for the owner or the manager to find out some facts about the rink. What year was it built? Who originally started it? Who owns it now? Do you have an Adult Night? Does your rink still have the old school stickers or patches? Tell me some history about the rink and any other questions I come up with while rolling at their rink. Then, I'll point out the problems I found in the rink and see when they are going to be addressed. About a week after I leave, I'll finish their review and post it to Facebook, Instagram, and Twitter. Then, down the road, I'll post any of the videos on YouTube. I also catalog and save everything in case something happens to that roller rink, so we have it for historical value or insurance if necessary.

I have been featured on YouTube, radio stations, podcasts, movies, videos, magazines, newspaper articles, TV news and the Roller Skating Association's Convention. You can find me in attendance at various roller skating events throughout the country such as Roller Derby, Speed Skating, Artistic, Skate parties, Adult Skates, Regular Sessions, Skate fundraisers, RSA Conventions, USARS aka USA Roller Sports and many others.

If you see me at your local Roller Rink measuring the Skate Floor I invite you to say, "Hi".

If you dare, join me on a skate trip. See if you can hang out with the Skate Critic. I generally wear people out. They usually quit the first day and opt to stay at the hotel for the rest of the trip. I've only had a few people go to more than one rink with me on a trip. And there's only one person that has been able to hang every day on several trips.

I also sell Roller Skates for Golden Horse Roller Skates, the artistic line out of our local rink Paradise Skate in Antioch, California under Paradiseskatewholesale.com. I am sponsored by Susan Geary of RollerSkater.com and always looking for more opportunities in the Skate World to pay for my "Hobby that's lost its mind!"

In closing, ask yourself what can you do to make the roller skating world a better place? I say, be yourself and watch what grows. You never know what you will become accidentally.

The Skate Critic Out!!!

ABOUT THE AUTHOR:

My name is Ginger Dawn Mathews. I am known in the Skate World as the Skate Critic. I travel around the world to review roller rinks. I post these reviews on several Social Media sites. I also keep track of all the live rinks and dead rinks in the US. I am a Freestyle/Rex Skater in the adult skate world. I come from a long line of skaters from many different avenues of the skate world.

Favorite Quote:

"Failure to plan on your part does not constitute an emergency on my part."

Facebook: @ginger.d.mathews @theSkateCritic

Instagram: @theskatecritic

To view videos of the author, grab the physical copy for an interactive experience.

Skatetronic

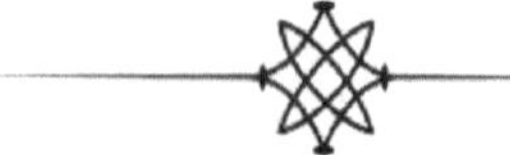

Michael Giles aka Diddy

My name is Michael Giles aka Mike Diddy from Petersburg, Virginia. It's a small town with a ton of history and a couple of major stars that have been born here. Some names like Moses Malone, Blair Underwood, and Trey Songz just to name a few. Even Martin Luther King Jr. used to visit Petersburg during the Civil Rights days. He was a major influence back then and helped create the opportunity to enjoy some of our freedoms today. Growing up here, I didn't know it was as small as it is.

I didn't have to go far to find out. For me, that thing was "roller skating." I've always had a thing for anything with wheels that I could be creative with. Now, when I say creative, I mean give it your own little twist of style.

Alongside your style, sometimes you have to bring competitive nature into the mix. What can I say? I'm a naturally competitive person. I think that's a normal feeling when you're adding style to anything. If it doesn't have any style, no one will notice. Whether or not you want to accept it, you too are a competitive person to a certain degree, especially when you care about being noticed by others.

I was an only child from my mother. Being an only child, I've always been more drawn to sports and hobbies where the results are based solely on my performance. The teammate relationship was always attractive to me. The part I have problems with is when teammates make mistakes and we all have to suffer for it. I know it sounds ass backwards that I enjoyed the brotherhood of the teammate experience and also hated the pain of it. This is what should make the win more satisfying, when you all accomplish something together...YES, I KNOW THIS ... Yet, it still bothers me. Well, at least I'm being honest.

I was born into a roller skating family. A lot of my direct family skated as kids and well into their adult years. Back in the 1980s, when my mother and I lived with my grandma, I can remember my cousins coming home from the skating rink, always having exciting stories about life in the rink. They would talk about music, the routines, and girls of course. They were all much older than me, having fun in their twenties, just as anyone would in that position. Naturally, I would beg them to take me.

They would just laugh, saying, "You're too young. Ask your mom to take you to the rink."

I had a lot of toys but life at the skating rink was a mystery to me as a kid. I knew my time would come. In the 1987-1988 school year, I heard a rumor that the second graders got a chance to go on a field trip to the Rollercade, our town's local Skating Rink. I had never seen the inside of it. The closest I had even been to it was in my mom's car, passing it on the way to the grocery store. I knew I was only about one year away from being able to go to the skating rink. In the 1988-1989 school year, when I reached the second grade, I got my opportunity.

Now that I think about it, I had to be a bit of an obsessed, detailed thinking, crazy kid to think like this at six or seven years old. I didn't go on that trip until I was eight in 1989. I knew that I had one shot to show my mom that I was serious for her to keep bringing me back. When I got my first shot to lace up my little brownies with orange wheels, I did it to the best of my little eight-year-old non-skating ability. I had no skill, but my drive was high. I remember catching on quickly and only holding the wall around a couple of times. The rest of the time at the rink was an absolutely amazing experience for me. From that day forward I've been addicted to roller skating, which was very much a staple in my life all the way through grade school. I was known as the kid that didn't go to the teen clubs at all. I went to the skating rink. My first job was in the skating rink. My first kiss from my childhood love was in the skating rink. I met my best friend in the skating rink. My skating partner, Jit, was in my second grade class in 1989 that went to the skating rink.

If you know me, I'm sure you know my friendship with Jit and our connection to roller skating are deeper than the Atlantic Ocean. I met Brandi, my wife of eleven years now, in the skating rink as an adult. Do you see the trend and commitment to the culture? I didn't just pick roller skating up. I was born into it and never stopped "implementing" it into my life.

As a pre-teen, I wasn't into the type of skating I'm into now. Due to lack of exposure, I didn't see much of that until I was able to attend the adult sessions years later. As a youth, I skated in speed skates at the local rink during 7pm to 11pm sessions on Saturday nights. If you were looking for me, you only needed to check your watch. I was going to be there without a doubt.

There was a Friday night session that also ran from 7pm to 11pm, which I did attend every once in a while. I only attended that session for a couple of reasons, and it certainly wasn't for social reasons or musical entertainment. None of the kids there went to my school or lived in Petersburg. They were only there because the Rollercade was the closest rink to the surrounding counties near Petersburg, where I lived. I went because that was the only night of the week that they raced on. The Saturday night session was called Soul Night aka Black Night. The Friday night session was just JAM Skating night that played Pop Music, Country, and Rock & Roll. I think it's safe to say if you heard three R&B or Rap records, you had a good night. I wasn't too concerned with that anyway because the racing was my main concern.

They would line the kids up by age groups and let us race. Even then, I didn't know I had the drive to be competitive. I just knew I found that part of skating exciting and if I studied the technique of the older skater kids, I would give myself a good chance of winning. The winner got free drinks from the snack bar, which was a big deal to me because I had to use part of my allowance to get in the session. A free drink to win was definitely greatly appreciated. It was great when I didn't have to use my own money in the rink to eat and drink at times. This was another reason later on, I got a job at the rink so I could eat and drink for free while skating on the job. The game was always chess not checkers.

When I graduated from High School in 1999, I began to hear about adult sessions in Richmond and Smithfield, VA. My friends and I started to attend the sessions as well as join the local club in Richmond called Richmond Soul Rollers. That club eventually turned into Virginia Skate Connection (VSC), which I was the youngest member at the time. The older members really took to us (Jit and me) and took care of us like we were their own children at times. I'll always love them for that. As we were entering the 2000s skating was really starting to catch fire. I was traveling to twenty to thirty parties a year plus my local sessions. Almost every weekend, it was another party in another state. My popularity was growing, alongside that of Virginia, which was gradually becoming a state with growing skate talent and sessions.

This was an important time before social media. We depended on www.Skategroove.com and www.Jivebiscuit.com for all our skate news and party schedule updates. Many skate media groups were creating online magazines, websites, and DVDs. I remember feeling amazed and disappointed the first time I saw myself on film. I was happy but wasn't impressed, knowing that I needed to work harder. Virginia was growing and migrating to the Smithfield as its main adult skate night hub. More relationships were being formed between (804) and (757) skaters throughout the state. Virginia, from that point on, transformed into what skaters enjoy today as a very rich skating community set up back then by Virginia Skate Connection.

Skating alliances between Richmond and the Tidewater area was such a big thing to me. As skaters, we all grew and attracted more attention to our state. We attracted so much attention that four skaters got filmed at a national party in Virginia by a Filmmaker named Tyrone Dixon. He had some success with a roller skating documentary that featured myself and many other skaters. He got a chance to film more skaters to potentially be cast in a major film. I was picked to be body double for the actor Brandon T. Jackson who played "Junior" in the Movie "Roll Bounce". Looking back at the experience, I appreciate it more now than I did then. Although it wasn't difficult in terms of skill. It was hard to learn the business. I learned a lot even though I was only twenty-four years old at that time.

At the time of writing this, I'm days away from being forty. I didn't have the business knowledge as the actors, who were part of S.A.G. (Screen Actors Guild). So, there were points during the filming, where I wasn't exactly happy and felt that I didn't understand enough of the business. I also felt we weren't being told enough to educate us on the business we were in. The money was good, and we were always paid. For some, that was good enough.

I got a bad reputation for asking questions. I always asked questions that benefited the group. I left my job to do the movie with permission and moved to Chicago for 3 months to shoot the Roll Bounce movie with less than a week's notice. That was a big gamble for me, which eventually cost me my job back home in Virginia. I wasn't a professional actor. I was a popular underground kid that skated for a professional actor. None of the skate doubles were paid beyond that last day on set. When Roll Bounce comes on TV now, I don't receive anything. So, you're fucking right! I ask questions because I learned how important residual income was at 24 years old. Follow your gut always and trust no one when it comes to money. Other than that, I enjoyed the experience very much. I will recommend to younger skaters that if they get the opportunity to ever do a commercial or movie to do it, just try to join S.A.G. Trust me, it will be to your benefit in the long run.

These days, as I've transitioned to being a husband and father, I still enjoy skating, remembering all the highlights, and people I've met. Some other highlights in skating for me have been when Red Bull Energy Drink sent me a couple of cases with a letter, telling me they enjoyed my skating videos on YouTube, although they just didn't have a market yet for roller skaters when I attempted to get signed by them. I'm thankful for Jaye Flynn, Irv Williams, Reggie Gunn as these were the main skaters that I built my style around. Lastly, thank you to Dwight "Cadillac" Dodson (VA) and the belated Michael Johnson (NY), who gave me confidence as a skater when I didn't see what they saw.

ABOUT THE AUTHOR:
Michael Giles aka Mike Diddy is from Petersburg, Virginia. He is one half of the legendary skate team known as the Dynamic Duo.

Facebook: @Mikediddy
Mikegiles: 7- Youtube

To view videos of the author, grab the physical copy for an interactive experience.

Dynamic Duo

Lawrence Thomas/Michael Giles aka Jit and Diddy

Hello skaters, my name is Lawrence 'Jit' Thomas better-known as 'Jit' from the Dynamic Duo with my partner Mike Diddy. Let's see, where can I start? 1996-1997 is where it all started for us as we were beginning to transition into skating more seriously. Our skating journey began in elementary school moving through to high school. We had a long stretch in developing our skills into what more accomplished skaters have seen over the years. It took a lot of practice hours and time out of the spotlight that many didn't see until our season in the spotlight came. In the beginning, we weren't even that great. But with practice anything is possible.

Together we accomplished things we never imagined would happen. Winning multiple Adrenaline Awards for several straight years was our biggest accomplishment as a unit. The awards committee retired us and declared that we were unable to win anymore. That felt a little unfair in the beginning but, over time we learned to take it as a compliment. With our youth and talent, we carried Virginia on our back from being the two young kids to the men we are today. A lot of the new skaters from VA don't know that. We highly encourage new skaters from anywhere on the globe, to be a student of their craft.

Please study and know your history! The way people skate today comes from us via a special inheritance to us from Jaye Flynn. Jaye was also Diddy's mentor and close friend at the time. He lived in the Tidewater area where we skated a lot and he was able to show us a lot of the style we skate today. That style is known as the 'Jammin Technique,' originating with Bill Butler. We were lucky enough to receive tapes of Bill Butler's top protege in New York to study. After we studied the tapes, we developed our styles with it, which is what the younger generation uses today. Some do know the history and some are just cocky—which is the sad part. Hopefully, in time they will learn to respect the artistry present here and its' history.

(Jit)

A lot of people don't know I'm a former dancer. I have even been on tours with professional singers and other dancers who you see on TV today. Being that I love music and dance routines, I guess roller skating has always felt like home to me. I live here in VA but a while ago I decided to move to Raleigh, NC. Upon arriving, I noted they skated JB a lot, so the style I skated was different from them when I moved there. They knew who I was, so it was natural that they wanted to learn the style. This is why a lot of skaters now in North Carolina are skating that style these days also. I didn't mind teaching which I still do a little presently.

(Jit)

Diddy and I both come from skate families. My mother was a skater and I followed in her footsteps. As a kid, I remember playing with her skates on the kitchen floor and trying to skate. Skating has always been with me. It's literally in my blood. I even have a tattoo with skates and laces on my arm. The style and culture are forever connected to me.

(Diddy)

A lot of people may not know this but, in the very beginning, Jit and I weren't partners. We had another friend who was skating with us. Jit and he were learning routines together. I just didn't have the interest at the time. Also, we weren't skating the Jammin Technique yet either so I didn't see the benefit yet. When we traveled down to the Smithfield skating rink in Smithfield, VA for the first time to their adult night, the excitement started to build. We were too young to get in and Debbie the rink owner had to give us special permission. Back then, Smithfield and other rinks had their following and star skaters. Cadillac, Junior, and Bryd were the 3-man team to beat. We were the scrubs. We looked up to them and stayed in their shadows for a while until we grew into our own. Our friend, the 3rd guy on our team went to the military leaving Jit and me to continue. We leaned on each other to learn the craft.

Dwight 'Cadillac' Dodson helped Jit and Me develop a lot. He had a small falling out in his group and asked did we want to join up with him. He was much better and older than us. In joining Dodson, we learned a lot about music, routines, break dancing, and even coordinating our outfits when we went out of town. Cadillac was a key player in helping us. Years later, Cadillac and Byrd also got an opportunity to be background extras in *Roll Bounce*. Getting on film was a huge opportunity in Virginia Beach at Haygood Skating Rink by Tyrone Dixon—who got me my role in the film. Through all of these events, Jit and I have grown a lot over the years.

There have been numerous people who have had a hand in each transition. Over the 20 plus years, we wish we could thank everyone personally. I hope this chapter is enough to show them we appreciated and took advantage of every skating milestone presented to us.

We'll see y'all on the wood!

ABOUT THE AUTHORS:

Lawrence 'Jit' Thomas and Mike 'Diddy' Giles have been skating together since the second grade. They are known in the skate world as the Dynamic Duo.

Facebook @mike.diddygiles @jit.thomas.1

To view videos of the author, grab the physical copy for an interactive experience.

Where Do We Go From Here?

Richard Houston aka Rockin Richard

My passion for roller skating started in the late 1950s and I became obsessed with it. I skated every opportunity that I could get out of the house, five or more days each week, two sessions most days. I wanted to learn everything I could and wanted to practice as much as I could. Watching and learning from some of the best senior skaters in the rink, practicing the moves over and over again until I mastered them. I had to work on smoothness and showmanship. Every wheel on your skates serves a purpose. When you perform a move, and another skater compliments you on that move and asks you to do that move again or asks you to teach it to them, then you know your skating skills are improving.

After working on moves over and over, I started to get a lot of skaters' attention. In the early 1970s, I started entering contests that we called Be-Bops, which were contests of skating skills on the rink floor. The best skaters won a trophy for first place, second place, or third place in categories such as Men's Singles, Ladies Singles, and Couples - men and women skating together. After winning a few Be-Bops, I started getting better at performing on skates. In 1979, I was watching a show on TV called The Gong Show, which featured people doing crazy things. I wanted to skate on the show and win that $500 Gong Show Trophy. I called NBC Studios in Hollywood and they gave me an audition date. Getting there was another thing. Flying was too expensive for me. I got on a Greyhound Bus and three days later (badly needing a shower), I was in Los Angeles, California (Hollywood Baby!). I arrived just 3 hours before my audition time. Friends were waiting for me at the bus station to take me to NBC Studios. After qualifying for the show, nothing was going to stop me from winning the show. Two weeks later, on the day of the show, I was a nervous wreck but ready to roll because I knew I couldn't go back to Detroit without that trophy, (and the cash, Ha! Ha!).

After Chuck Barris introduced me, the curtain opened, and everyone was watching me. That was another out-of-body experience and all I kept thinking was, 'Feet, don't fail me now.'

After winning The Gong Show on roller skates in 1979, I returned to The Gong Show stage that same year as a paid guest performer, which excited the hell out of me. Meeting celebrities at NBC studios who appreciated what I was doing on skates and knowing that they also roller skated had me on a cloud that was never going to fade out. Every skater, who accomplished something on skates that took them to another level, knows what I'm talking about.

I had the opportunity to open for James Brown in Detroit in 1985 in a fashion show and concert on Woodward Ave and Grand Blvd. You should have seen me modeling on wheels. Remember what I just said, 'Modeling on Wheels', coming soon to a rink or club. After the show, I was walking past James Brown's dressing room and as I was leaving the venue, he called out to me to come into his dressing room.

He said that was one of the best jamming on skates he had seen in a long time and it looked like I was having fun. First, it took me a few seconds to gather myself. Here was the Godfather of Soul talking to me and telling me that he saw me skating and was impressed with it.

I said, "I feel alive when I'm skating. Being in control of the wheels also makes you show off with a feeling of I GOT THIS."

Then he said, "Keep doing it until it's not fun anymore. Then, you stop."

That was a great motivation for me to keep rolling every chance I could, after hearing that from James Brown, The Godfather of Soul, The Hardest Working Man in Show Business. Something I will remember for the rest of my life. Rest in heaven James Brown.

If you were not at the Legends in the Sky Skating Party on November 2, 2019, in Washington D.C., in a building, thirty-one floors up, you missed a high that is going to take a long time for me to recover from. Roller skating on the thirty-first floor surrounded by two hundred 12-foot-tall glass windows, skaters dressed in formal wear while sipping on champagne and eating hors d'oeuvres and listening to Vaughan Mason sing "Bounce, Rock, Skate, Roll" live. That just made my night perfect. That night was the last time Vaughan Mason performed live for skaters. Vaughan Mason received his skating wings on April 4, 2020. Rest in heaven Vaughan Mason, your song will be remembered forever.

That was just the start of the type of skating parties we are going to be presenting to the world because technology has caught up with our talents (about time!). We are in for a treat next year and for years to come. We must leave everything we have for the younger skaters following our footsteps. No matter what city you are from or the type of style you have, we must stay different to be able to learn from one another, to keep new styles forming that will have us skating forever. That's the key to this puzzle of skating. That is how I learned different moves from watching other skaters doing their thing. You take that move and go into your rolodex of moves that you have in your head and find a place for it, when you hit the wood or whatever surface you're skating on. I can watch skaters perform all day long and come up with a book of moves to learn from. That is why we need each other to pass it down.

Now, let me try to explain what age twenty-five and over, or age thirty and over Old School and New School means to me. This is just my observation from watching skaters over fifty years old, going in circles, doing things that still amaze me. This means that no matter how many times you go skating, you will see a skater performing something different. Going to skating parties happening all over the country is so much fun attending. The problem comes when someone asks what is age eighteen and over, or age twenty-five and over. The stated age range tells a skater if they are going to the party or not.

The number one reason for attending the party or not, due to the stated age range, is because of the music. Back in the days, the entire family went skating and listened to the same music. Now, all that has changed. We have Rap and Hip-Hop for the young skaters (New School), some older skaters also enjoy it. R & B and Jazz is for the older skaters (Old School). The different music genres make it extremely hard for a DJ to make everyone happy. Older skaters sometimes want to move slower and glide to the smooth beats coming from the Whispers, or The O'Jays. Younger skaters want a faster beat to go ninety miles an hour. They need to burn that energy off and R & B is not going to cut it.

The skating party hosts should follow the example of Joi in Atlanta. Joi had a thirty and over session for the adult skaters from 9pm to 12am followed by a 12am to 5am session for eighteen or twenty-one and over. The DJ loved her for it. Some thirty and over skaters will stay to enjoy skating longer; some will do a Meet and Greet, shop the vendors or skate again if they hear a beat they like. Most of all, you will have everyone in the building to share old and new things about skating. Vendors will be able to sell more goods and services related to skating. Older skaters may teach the younger skaters. And the younger skaters, who are serious about becoming better, will listen to what they have to say. When you come to a thirty and over skating party, you are surrounded by professionals - Doctors, Lawyers, Police, the list goes on and on.

We don't have time for insecure skaters. You can check that at the door. We don't have time for skaters that can't handle their girlfriend or boyfriend skating with someone or talking to someone. It's a grown folks party. Or skaters who want to fight you because you bumped into them by accident, we don't have time for that. We went to Chicago to a thirty and over skating party at the rink from 10am to 2pm, skaters were coming in with suitcases containing ballroom shoes to dance in, cards to play bid whist, chess boards, ping pong paddles. These are some of the things an eighteen and over party will not have.

There's a code you must live by to become a thirty and over skater. You must know how to talk on our websites, Facebook, and skating shows among others. Our goal is to pass our talents on to anyone and everyone, who wants to learn and have fun along the way. When it comes to skating, all you have to do is ask. I get a lot of joy when I see someone hitting one of the moves that I created (only a Real Skater is going to understand what I just said).

To all the SKATERS we have lost because of this Pandemic and other causes, my prayers go out to all the families. We have lost some skating styles that we will never, I mean NEVER, see again and that's a shame. We must and will have a tribute for all the skaters that we have lost during this crisis that held us back for over a year from having bigger and better skating parties. We love skating so much that we will skate on anything smooth (indoors or out). The skating coverage from the press during this pandemic is a testament to our love for skating and the thousands of skaters, who have joined the movement to catch that thrill on wheels.

We must be smart during this pandemic and wear a mask, wash, and sanitize hands, and maintain social distancing so that we can roll through this setback. It won't be long now. We have come too far to rollback now.

Take this time to think about all the new things we can do and when the time is right, bring it to life. This is one big party and if we roll it right, the sky's the limit. Skating has fulfilled so many things in my life. My health is amazing, which is at the top of the list of benefits from skating. My kids … sorry, my grown kids' health is great because they skate also. One of my sons, Greg, even fastens his skates in a seatbelt in the front seat of his vehicle on his way to the skating rink to keep his skates safe. One of my joys in life is seeing Greg skate and develop a style of his own as well as watching him skate with different skaters and learning the style of other skaters. He also likes it when we skate together. His eagerness to learn from everyone is helping him become a better skater.

I will end by saying this to every skater: Enjoy the ride. It will pay off in more ways than you can imagine.

ABOUT THE AUTHOR:

Richard Houston aka Rockin Richard has been skating since the late 1950s.

Facebook: Rockin Richard Houston

To view videos of the author, grab the physical copy for an interactive experience.

My Skating Journey

Myesha McCaskill aka Smooth Goddess

My skating journey's cultivation has unfolded for the past twenty-eight years. I began skating at the solid age of ten. There was one particular day I remember riding on the expressway with my mother when I saw a skating rink passing nearby. I informed my mother that I would like to go skating at that particular rink. She purchased me a pair of rollerblades, and shortly thereafter—the rest became history! A lot of people don't know I started with roller blades before eventually switching to quads. When I finally started skating at the rink, I noticed all of the other kids had roller skates and I thought that was the coolest thing! So, I told both of my parents that I wanted roller skates for Christmas. When I finally got my first pair of roller skates, I would go skating every single Saturday in Gurnee, IL. My mother, eventually, let me know that she had to move back to Chicago because she was taking up new employment. I was extremely saddened because I had met a lot of cool and wonderful people at the surrounding rinks and at my current school at that time.

At the age of twelve, I went to The Rink Chicago; this particular skating rink eventually became my new home. The Rink Chicago became the center where a lot of my gifts and talents flourished and cultivated. The JB style of skating found me at the age of twelve. I admired a lot of Old School Skate Pioneers, such as Duane Hibler and Derrick Lewis. I used to watch their feet, trying to imitate their movements and worked on comprehending my understanding of their movements while grooving in Hyde Skates. Since then, I began self-teaching myself! I learned how to develop my way of skating so that I could upgrade my skillset to rise above the rest of the competition. I became a cultured self-taught skater from the ages of ten to twenty-five years old. During my twenties, I was able to become a part of an amazing female skate group formerly known as the 'Center of Attention,' headed by Paris White. Amongst this group, I was able to skate with women based out of Chicago, Florida, and Atlanta. When I turned twenty-five years old, I began to branch off learning from amazing mentors along my solo journeys such as Josh 'Bat Smoke' Smith who taught me groundwork; then Calvin, who taught me to balance, control, and the art of basic spins. Finally, it was Elon King Eway who brought it home for me and taught me musicality, JB Skate Style, level of difficulty in advanced movement, and how to hone in on developing a transitional combination of move sequences. In other words, he taught me how to put a series of moves together and to make it to where even the best of skaters won't be able to understand the technique!!! If you don't believe me, just go ask Bobby West (hahaha)!

Growing up at The Rink Chicago landed me my first job as a skate guard, where I also did double-duty working as a cashier in the ticket office. The former rink owners, Carmen and Nate gave me my first job at the age of 16 and I will always be grateful to them for teaching me the art of community work in the skate culture, which is why I am so passionate about teaching skating and working for the community. Going away to college didn't stop my skating. I would come back on many holidays ready to skate. My first skate jam was in 2012, located in North Carolina, where my introduction to other skate styles and cultures caught fire. I was so amazed at the other styles that were as significant and distinguished as the JB skate style. This was a true learning experience.

From that very moment, I realized I wanted to become better at skating and become more diverse at it, so that I could be able to skate to all types of music and connect, through skating, with other out of town skaters. I realized the only way to do that was to broaden my horizons and diversify my craft. I started to practice other skate styles and that's when God began to open doors and connect me with elite skaters from different cities. These connections greatly influenced me—one, in helping to improve my skill levels; and two —presenting myself on many different platforms.

I consider my native skate style to be a JB skater, but I'm also a diverse skater who does more than just one JB skate style. From this point on, I entered into several national competitions and showcased my gifts and talents. Being featured in the *United Skates' Documentary,* and also in various episodes of the television series *The Chi* for two seasons—allowed my platform to grow. Also, a skate catalog entitled *Introducing Your Favorite Skater Vol. 2*, continued my streak of features in this arena of skating.

God has truly been a blessing to me, and His blessings never stopped with me just learning to skate. The Lord took my passion for skating and allowed me to expand and further challenge myself by beginning to teach. I'm currently teaching skate instructional classes every Saturday at Glenwood Roller Rink located in Glenwood, IL. Since I've started teaching, the gift that God has given me has placed me on a platform to create an organization called 'Inspired by Favor.' The name I chose for the organization INSPIRED BY FAVOR, was born out of the favor of God, and His inspiration in me to create this platform to teach and serve the Chicagoland area. I have amazing instructors who assist me with the classes every Saturday and my weekly reward is the opportunity to watch them succeed and pour their passion for skating into others, in turn, giving back to the community.

I hope that my story can empower other skaters to understand that with God's favor, all things are possible.

With hard work and dedication, your dreams can become YOUR REALITY!

ABOUT THE AUTHOR:

Myesha (Smooth Goddess) McCaskill was born on January 1, 1983. She is the product of a single parent home that was full of love, motivation, and inspiration. Even though Myesha faced down many tough obstacles, she never let anything stop her from accomplishing her dreams and goals.

Helping her surrounding communities via the advocation of fitness for the youth and adults of Chicago McCaskill kept working hard on her goals.

A fine graduate of Dixon Elementary School in the year 1997, Myesha went on to graduate from Washington High School in 2001; where she became an active member of the basketball and cross-country team. Myesha served as an inspiration to all of her fellow teammates and classmates while earning several awards through her sports activities.

Ms. McCaskill continued her education at Rust College and graduated with a Bachelors Degree of Science with a concentration in Biology. Along with her studies, Myesha became an active member of one of the finest sororities, Alpha Kappa Alpha.

Although proud of everything she had done so far, Myesha's most prized accomplishment is competing for a course of study and seminars to receive her license to be an Elder in the Rhema Word Ministries under the leadership of Pastor Kenneth Hagen. She delivered her first sermon and was ordained on January 23, 2005. God knew this destiny would follow her life, and in preparation, this young lady served as school chaplain her freshmen through senior years at Rust.

Myesha McCaskill, now 38 years of age, has developed her love of skating and fitness through hard work and dedication for the last 28 years. While displaying her gift and talents in the original Chicago JB Skate Style, Myesha went onto feature in two seasons of *The Chi* and was featured in one of the greatest skate documentaries *UNITED SKATES DOCUMENTARY*. Myesha has earned numerous national awards for competing in different national skate events across the country. Myesha's motivation and drive to push the Chicago skate culture forward through fitness stems from years of adversity to learn, understand and perfect the Chicago JB Style.

If You Ain't Sweatin You Ain't Workin

India Bernadino aka Engine

The Crew with different skills. We love what we do on skates. Philadelphia - the love we have for our city is unreal. Philadelphia is known to be the city of brotherly love, but wait, don't get it twisted. There can be rough egos out here sometimes. Our crew, Great on Skates, is passionate about the arts and focuses on our culture to build up our community.

You can find different things in the city for inspiration. Our team is a dope family with different backgrounds and performance abilities. Would you believe that we are not all skaters? Some members are known for their previous passions such as playing the drums, dancing, miming, singing, djing, break dancing, teaching, and theatre performances. These are all gems that made Great on Skates become a thing!

Ever since I can remember, I've been following the footsteps of my father (Master Jay, James Bruno) about teaching and creating. My Father was both a dancer and a roller-skater, who has lots of experience sharing his passion and gift of performing in front of others.

Now, the torch is currently in my hands to continue to make people smile through roller dance. My first love has always been dancing and theatre. While facing my life changes, I looked to skating as an uplifting best friend. I met Shamar Cunningham, who is like-minded and very genuine. Sometimes, I stay up all night thinking of our next idea to conquer on wheels. Most ideas have been inspired by the group's many talents. We've learned that the best place to capture the hearts of those who aren't skaters is expanding our radius outside of the skating rink. We hope you like what you see so far!

Skating has been known to uplift those in a state of sadness, depression, defeat, and more. I can speak about this personally as I was one of the above. My great grandmother, who was everything to me, was losing her life. And boy! The tears were my skates. I know that may sound weird but, because of skating, I still haven't cried. Losing someone is not easy but finding something that feels like an endless love, known to me as skating, has changed my life and patched up a wounded space.

"Ricky" introduces me to the Miraculous

Ricky, Richard Evans, my best friend is better known as "Glytch" brought me out to the rink. I would see him videotaping himself and posting footage of going around the rink alone. I thought, "Wow he looks free, he's loving it, and he's out there by himself."

Once he invited me out to the rink, he told me, "You gotta meet Shamar better known as 'Miraculous Spinz', he skates his butt off."

Once I saw him spin, I dropped my skate bag and my jaw. I immediately realized that I was going to be a frequent visitor. I never would have thought that we would form a company of individuals who just love to perform. To this day, Miraculous is one of our greatest mentors. "Hungry Ray" and "Philly Nuke" became a part of the team. We also had Rachel Snider "HUNGRY FOR ALL THINGS" as well as Antwine Holder "The Quiet One". There's always room for more when you have talent. Hungry Ray is the perfect definition of no fear lives here. She has been in the circle of dance arts with me and Ricky for many years. I first discovered Ray on skates around 2017 at my studio in South Philadelphia. At the time, we were just having these roller dance classes with my father before we started to play around on the skates. I never took heed to skating, even at that time. I was so focused on my dance making a living out of my passion.

My father was a dancer on skates. I saw him pick Ray up in the air and just skate with her so confidently. She's one of a kind, who can be up for any challenges on wheels.

What can I say about Philly Nuke that won't make me laugh? He is a character of suspense, confidence, speed, laughter, and boldness at the same time. I've witnessed Nuke in rare form when we've perform together. I like the fact that he is always ready to be a leader and team player. Shamar had always spoken so highly of Nuke before he joined us. At rehearsals, I would laugh because he would freeze up when it was time for Shamar solos as if he were one from the outside looking in.

My inner self was always screaming at Antwine saying, "You're on the same show with us."

I like the fact that he is always wowed at what we do as a whole. Antwine is the skater of the crew, whose favorite style is fast backward, trains, and trios.

Slow Walk Toot (Courtenay Elder) became a part of the team when he wanted to audition for a singing/roller skating part in an upcoming Skate Musical. This was how "Slow Walk Toot" became a part of 'Great on Skates'. Right away, she had the energy and creativity that complimented a lot of the team. After a few weeks, we all got to witness Toots' other talents. She brings a different character to the group. Courtenay has a passion for miming, which is a different artistic expression. We love the fact that she can incorporate this with her skating.

We asked the Crew, "How does it feel to be of the New Generation of skaters?"

Courtenay Elder (Slow Walk Toot): "How it feels to me to be the next generation of skaters is magnificent, fantastic, exciting! I'm so glad to be a part of this new generation. As a new generational skater, I still give honor to those who have sweated, worked hard, practiced day and night to create moves so I may keep those moves alive. I feel it is important to continue the legacy of roller dance, freestyle, jam skate, and more. For me, this newer generation doesn't have just one style. We are creative in our way. Though this is an exciting time to be a part of this new generation of skating, it has its challenges of being welcomed into the skate world."

"The key, is to stay true to your style, be you, and don't worry about what others think. Stay positive and continue to support your skate community and your rink as you encourage others to learn and always give back by teaching to keep roller skating alive in the community!"

Rachel Snider (Hungry Ray): "I'm not sure how it feels. I do it because I enjoy it. There are people that I look up to that are deeply rooted in the skate culture. I look up to them and what they've done. I just enjoy being a part of it. I want to learn as much as I can to pass on to future generations. It's inspiring even to ask a beginner or intermediate skater. There are always people watching, looking up to you. I want to be the most authentic version of what skate culture is, to the best of my ability. It should never be watered down for people, and that's how the roots will stay strong. It's good when OG skaters are hard on you and don't give you props. It makes it much more valuable when they finally do. There's a huge responsibility to keep the culture and respect all the work and history that people put into it."

Antwine Holder (Philly Nuke): "It's a challenge being the next-gen skater. We get to see the best of the best, along with the upcoming ones. This is also the era of social media, where skaters get to connect with one another without ever actually meeting physically. It's also the movement of influencers. Watching the young skaters do and imitate who they idolize is great for the community. It carries on the tradition and specific styles."

"Along with the good comes the bad, though. We also have to deal with what may be the most segregated time of skating as well. A lot of people feel that just because they don't do the same style, they can't work together, and that causes separation. This is why it's difficult to collaborate with a lot of people."

India Hyman Bernardino (Engine): "I'd like to say that is the next generation of skaters has its ups and downs. If you are going to stay at a certain level confined to the wood, then it may be an okay experience. I've surrounded myself with people, who want to do more with the dreams they have. I believe that whatever goals you have should never be stopped because of anyone or anything. Just like any community or block, you always have the bully or the one you have to be careful of for no reason at all. Why, what's the issue? Why are you so angry? Why do you not share the knowledge you have? Why do you gossip? Is this because you did not pursue your dreams? What is it that you are lacking that would make you discourage others?"

"Growing up, we were taught that respect should always be given to others, not just those before you, but respect others in general. We're not disrespectful to those who came before any of us. Even though some of us may be a little younger and have goals, we don't have to stop trying to achieve them because someone older than us has an issue. I'd like to say that it is hard for a new or next generation to come into this place called the skate world and move around in it (at least for me)."

"At first, it seems like the rink is a magical place where you find almost everyone is inviting, pleasant and supportive. Then, you find out that's not always the case. I wish I could tell everyone that everything is peaches and cream, but for those who love to be inspired and teach others, you should know about the red flags in the skating rinks. Let's meet at the rink, which is a place for us to gather and have fun. We meet there and lace-up. For most of us, it's the highlight of our day or week. For some, it's their second home."

What is Great on Skates about?
"Great on Skates" is an all-around skate community in Philadelphia, full of freedom, love, and family on skates. They incorporate dance with skating as well as spinning, tricks, fast backward, train & trios, and more. You can always find them skating at huge festivals, school assemblies, hosting skate events, and theater projects. These live performances bring child-like joy to the audience. This local skate community is led and driven by these great instructors Shamar Cunningham, India Bernardino, and Richard Evans. "Great on Skates" consists of teaching, training, and reaching on all levels. They are here as an outlet to your fear on wheels. You can find them putting their number one love into action, teaching the basics of balance, movement, control, and more on skates. "Great on skates" provides many classes in the Philadelphia area. You will be excited to learn how fast you will become "Great on Skates".

To view videos of the author, grab the physical copy for an interactive experience.

Becoming Buckwild

James Rich aka BuckWild

I will never forget that day in 1982, I was walking from the water after boogie boarding nice waves at Venice Beach with my best friends from high school. In the distance, I heard music playing. Being the music lover that I was, I naturally gravitated towards it. I came around a huge wall and there they were, the Venice Beach Skaters, skating on a path that led to what was then the Damson Oil Facility. As I got closer, I was amazed.

I had skated before, I'd played hockey when I was twelve, but I had never seen anything like this. Grown men dancing on roller skates. There was MAD, Terrell, Kyle, Shawn, and several others, who are still close friends of mine to this day, grooving to the latest rap and R&B sounds that I loved. I was mesmerized. All the way home, I couldn't stop talking to my friends about this artistic gift I had witnessed. I wanted to try it, but I didn't have any skates. As the thoughts of what I had seen that day started to fade by night, I was approached by one of my good friends, who had listened to me rant and rave all day about the roller skaters.

Out, from behind his back, came a pair of blue suede skates with big yellow wheels, yellow laces, and yellow stripes down the side. My eyes lit up.

He said to me, "Try these on. See if they fit."

I couldn't get them on fast enough. They fit me like a glove. It felt like they were meant for me. At that moment, my life changed. I could hardly sleep that night.

When I woke up the next morning, I headed to Venice Beach, excited to see if I still had a tidbit of the skills I had possessed as a hockey skating kid.

I walked up to the skate path and there they were as if they had never left. These skaters were in their element, grooving to one of my favorite songs, "So Fine" by Howard Johnson. I put on my new brightly colored used skates and stepped out on the skate floor. Whoop! I hit the deck.

I could have walked away and ended my career before it even got started, but being as determined as I was, I got right back up and took my first baby steps as a Venice Beach Skater. The rest is history.

It took me years to master certain moves that were well respected in the skate world. Sit spins, crazy legs, alphas, and windmills, just to name a few. But my passion truly became choreography. Throughout the years, my friends and I came up with routine after routine. Some, we used for professional shows we performed for thousands of people, and others were just for the spectators at Venice Beach. That was my favorite audience. The people that came from all around the world that seemed to live vicariously through us. They would watch us flow on wheels for hours, in amazement, as we freestyled and performed our choreographed hip-hop routines.

Skating has opened many unexpected doors for me, helping me launch several careers. Before I knew it, I was booking gigs. As time went by, I got better and ended up doing commercials for several products, including Pepsi. I also performed in music videos for various artists, and all kinds of shows, from corporate events to bar mitzvahs. I would take almost any gig that was willing to pay me for this gift that I had been blessed with. I even ended up modeling for seven years, gracing billboards, magazines, and runways. As a solo skater and as a part of various skating crews, I've blessed stages as an opening act for concerts, done tours teaching people how to skate, and have been able to travel all over the world without spending a dime of my own money.

Eventually, my skate family and I became Venice Beach celebrities. Still to this day, people approach me and tell me how they have been watching us skate for years. Some are inspired to put on skates and join the fun. Others are satisfied by watching us while they hang with friends or have lunch.

One of my favorite projects that I was able to be a part of is the skating documentary *Roller Dreams*, which tells the history of the Venice Beach Roller Skaters, and the struggle we've gone through to have our designated skate spot - The Venice Beach Skate Dance Plaza. We went from fighting for a strip of the sidewalk to skate on to having a professionally poured concrete surface made especially for roller skating.

Throughout the years, I've formed amazing relationships with fellow skaters and tourists from all over the world and visited them in their natural habitats and skating rinks. I have so many stories, it's hard to tell them all. From Europe to Asia to Mexico to islands all around the world, I've been able to see different styles of skating that have blown my mind.

My skate style has evolved throughout the years and I've had many nicknames from Duct-Tape-Jimmy to Organized Confusion to The Skating Tornado, but the one that stuck with me the most was BuckWild. I've received a wide range of comments from people, with some saying that I looked totally out of control, while others were saying that I was one of the wildest skaters they had ever seen. Some thought I looked like I was falling, but I would surprise them by turning the fall into another move, pulling from my large library of moves. I've had people say they thought I was about to hurt myself only to later recognize that it was just my style of skating. It's been said that I flow on skates like water. From a freestyle so smooth that it looked rehearsed to advanced choreographed routines, I was doing what only a handful of skaters could do. That's right! I can keep my *ass* off the ground and look good doin' it. I have become one of the most versatile skaters around and known by some of the most amazing skaters in the world.

I have been watched by some of the biggest celebrities in the world, but one of my favorite moments was when Debbie Allen, a famous dance choreographer, approached me after watching us skate for a while. She told me that she had done every kind of dance there was. She explained that this was one of the most amazing kinds of dance she had seen and that it was one she was going to leave to us. We both laughed respectfully.

In the last year, skating has exploded. I have been blessed to watch the incredible worldwide surge of new skaters taking to the concrete. For so long, outdoor skating was in a decline. It may not have always been apparent but skating never died. Skating has been alive in rinks all around the world. These rinks have continued to house some of the most amazing skaters in the world and now that the pandemic has shut down so many rinks, skaters have been forced to skate elsewhere, taking over basketball courts, tennis courts, outdoor hockey rinks, parking lots, and anywhere else they can find a flat smooth surface. This has brought visibility to skating; skaters now have an audience they never could have had before with rink admission fees. Add social media outlets like Facebook, Instagram, and TikTok to the scene, the whole world is now watching roller skaters. Skaters used to be hidden away in rinks or at places like Venice Beach, where you had to see them live and up-close. This phenomenon has been a huge part of the reemergence of roller skating, one of the fastest-growing sports in a long time. Getting a pair of skates has almost become impossible, with incredible wait times for the skates that are out of stock. New skate makers have started to pop up and seasoned skate companies have had to expand their manufacturing process like they never imagined.

When it was time for me to upgrade from my first pair of brightly colored hand-me-down skates, I turned to skate exclusively in Riedell's. I take skating seriously and I would only consider the best skating manufacturer for my skates. You wouldn't run a race in flip flops. That's how I feel about my skates.

Blood, sweat, and tears are what I put into my skating. It has kept me young, vibrant, and strong as well as in and out of trouble. Skating is an amazing exercise unlike any other; you work out muscles you don't normally use, and your balance, stamina, and strength are all tested on the skate floor. Trying to keep yourself off the floor is always motivation to get better at this sport. I have torn my medial meniscus as well as wrecked my back, but nothing has stopped me from lacing up. Every time I put on skates, I put my body at risk. I've seen broken bones, compound fractures, busted knees, cracked skulls, knocked out teeth, broken noses, and many other injuries. You would think that would have stopped me from ever putting skates on again, but I'm so addicted to skating that I'm willing to risk my life on the regular. Why? Because when I'm skating, I'm having the time of my life.

To me, music is a gift that has been with me throughout my life, from singing solos in my church choir as a six-year-old, singing opera in college, and becoming a signed hip hop artist in 1990. Music is the main reason I took to skating so easily. My love for dance has been in my DNA since birth. My love for skating has been with me since I played hockey with my buds as a kid. Put my love for music, my love for dance, and my love for skating together and you get one of the most skilled dance skaters in the world. After thirty-nine years and over twenty thousand hours of skating, I have put in the hard work to demand respect and to be considered an expert in the field.

No matter what race, religion, or age you are, skating can be for you. It is not prejudiced; it is accepting and non-biased. Skating is something you can do with a crowd of people or something you can do all by yourself. You can compete or you can do it recreationally. You can get as good as you want through hours of practice or you can putt-putt around occasionally just to clear your head. It is totally up to you. If you take to it, it is welcoming and challenging. It will test you to your core and make you realize that you are greater than you think. It will push you to be great and stretch your thinking. It will teach you to trust yourself and believe in yourself. When you nail that new move through the practice, master a routine, or even choreograph your own, you'll see what you're capable of. Skating is hard. It's strenuous. It's gruesome. It's tough. It's backbreaking and tedious but if you get good at it, you will have accomplished something amazing.

I encourage anyone and everyone to try skating at least once in their life. It will be one of the most challenging and rewarding things you will have ever tried. For some, it will come easy and for others, it will be the hardest thing they have ever tried. On some days, I put my skates on and I'm immediately in a zone. Other days, I put them on and can't balance to save my life. Every day is different. Every day is a toss-up. Consistently putting them on can only make the good days outweigh the bad ones.

Skating is my love. It is my all-time favorite activity. I go skating at least two to four days a week. When I'm lonely, I go skating. When I'm full of energy, I go skating. When I want to hang out with close friends or meet new ones, I go skating. When I need to clear my mind of worries, I go skating. I look for every reason to put on my wheels. I look for every reason to choreograph a new routine. I get excited when I'm going skating. When I am bored with work all week and a skate session is right around the corner, I crave skating like an addictive drug, like a lover I can't wait to see, like my favorite food I can't wait to eat, like the release from an intense workout. It is my serenity, my freedom, my healer, my religion. My escape. My true love. It helps me soar. Skating is life to me.

My love for skating has taught me many things. One of them being that if you do something long enough you will get good at it. I use this theory in everything I pursue. All aspects of my life have benefited from the hard work and dedication skating has inspired in me. I've gotten my film production degree as well as a culinary certification. I've started successful businesses, worked for companies like Patina Restaurant Group and BET, and worked with celebrities like Shaquille O'Neil, LL Cool J, Cicely Tyson, Babyface, and hundreds more. I'm a licensed Armed Security Guard and Certified Quality Insurance Officer. I now own income-generating real estate and continue to find ways to keep my financial independence, so it is possible to go skating whenever I want. I am grateful for being born in Los Angeles, CA, and to live on Venice Beach because it is such a special place in my heart and has become such an important part of who I am.

I am extremely blessed.

Skating will always be an integral part of my life and has done so much for me that now I want to spread the love through teaching. I love teaching choreography from beginning to advanced routines, as well as individual moves. My mission is to teach as many people as I can how to skate and to become Legends like myself. Why? Because as it says on my logo…

"Legends Are Made, Not Born"

-BuckWild

I Am The Greatest

Berri Blanco aka Strawberry Perez

June 1974, playing with cousins
"Who you're gonna be when you grow-up?'
Cousin1*: "I'm gonna be a person that cares for animals"...*
Cousin2*: "I'm gonna have a big house with lots of money (Not a profession*
but...lol)
Strawberry Perez*: I'M GONNA BE A MOVIE STAR!*

A Star was born. I am Berri Blanco aka Strawberry Perez! I was born and raised in New York City, The Bronx. Home of HipHop & "FLYizm". Growing up in New York was the best. The Music, Culture, Fashion, and, of course, Roller Skating.

August 1980, twelve years old, my mother took me to this building off of twenty-third street in Manhattan. Downstairs there was a lounge, but upstairs … "MAGIC". As a punishment, she told me to go upstairs until she finished up with friends. I walked upstairs towards my punishment. All I could say was, "WOW!"

The music, the ambiance, the roller skates. The best punishment ever! I always tried to get in trouble so she could take me back there. Once she saw how much fun I was having, she switched tactics. I kept roller skating from that day on. Throughout my years, circumstances and situations lead me to a different path. Nevertheless, my heart was always at the "rink".

I'm just starting to realize that when you disconnect from your true self and your bliss, you will endure hardship, pain suffering, but it can be short-lived. That process is to get back on course and live out your dream.

May 2015, I moved to Atlanta. As soon as I arrived, I was graced by the presence of the one and only Mr. Bill Butler. You think PRINCE has an Aura ... Mr. Bill Butler's talks, skating, overall presence are from another world. I started to attend his class. I didn't fully understand his "Jammin" technique so practicing was essential because I knew this was something great. I was learning and I wanted to be the best! And I was right!

One night, at an event, a guy walked up to me with his phone in hand and said: "Hello. This is you on my phone and my website. I am the president of Skatesus, and I would like to sponsor you! Call me!"

Yes! I am a National Sponsored Roller Skater with Edea Skates, Rolling & Skates! Still to this day.

Fast forward to the present. The year 2020, I was interviewed by the lovely and spiritual delight, Amirah Palmer. Jokingly, I suggested to her she needs some "Skate Entertainment" on her Podcast. Shortly after the interview, we talked and shared a few ideas. One idea turned us into skate conglomerates, creating skate apparel, writing books, hosting events and the list continues. I went from skating as a child to moving to Atlanta where I learned roller skating from the best. Now I have sponsorships, teach skate classes (Skate Finesse), own a skate clothing line (Juci Fruit), have performed at the biggest and best roller skating events to date. Recently, I've been a guest on the #1 Roller Skate podcast (Sk8rz Konnect!).

Now, the expansion of Berri Blanco Entertainment is here! I've truly woken up. My life inspires me every day. And I feel so honored to be in the skate world where I can use my voice and do all the skate greatness I do. Stay tuned! The Expansion of STRAWBERRY PEREZ continues.

"As I enter in towards the "Rink", my confidence grows. Once I enter the Skate floor, I'm a GOD!".... ~BERRI BLANCO

To view videos of the author, grab the physical copy for an interactive experience.

Skating Success

Eric Alston

I've always skated; I seriously can't remember not skating. I went for the first time on a Sunday, November 13, 1966, to be exact, the day before my fourth birthday, to Empire Rollerdrome in Brooklyn. My mom took me at least once a month until I could go there on my own with my sisters and friends from my neighborhood around the age of ten. We moved to Queens in May of 1977, and in August of 1978, Saint Albans Roller Rink opened eight blocks from my house.

It was a serious trek getting to Brooklyn to skate, and I was elated to have a much closer option. The last Sunday of that month was my first time seeing adults skate because prior to that I had only been to family sessions. There, I saw a guy named Derrick Williams couple skate with Sally Robinson, and I was instantly hooked. I was determined to learn how to skate like that! I didn't understand the magnitude of the moment, but it was the absolute genesis of my love of skating. I returned the next night, and I have never been off my skates for longer than two weeks since. I attended every single adult session there for an entire year until they closed for a month to redo the floor after a pipe burst. During that time, I ventured out and proceeded to do what I do today, finding new places to skate, meeting new people, connecting with new energies, and discovering styles, moves, wheels, boots, cities, states, and countries.

I currently reside in Atlanta, which has become the true mecca of our art, because every major style of skating is well represented here. This period has become skate nirvana for me, as we have skating seven days a week and multiple rinks, where we can roll at sessions that are well attended with a live DJ. During the era of Covid, we are one of the most fortunate areas in the world to be able to engage in our passion virtually unimpeded, and for that,

I'm eternally grateful.

I owe skating a debt I can never truly repay. Skating kept me off the streets and out of trouble, it contributes to the great health I've been blessed with, it's given me a respite during some of the most turbulent periods of my life, introduced me to friendships that I've been in all of my adult life, and placed me in contact with some of the most impactful individuals I have ever met. Skating has allowed me to become a mentor, coach, and trusted confidant to some of the most talented, promising, and enterprising young people within our culture.

Success means the progressive realization of a worthy ideal to me. I'm witnessing the evolution of skating. I have contributed to leaving things better than I found them. I feel I have honored our predecessors and those who have poured into me in the process.

Chicago At Heart

Bron Savage

I began my skating journey in December of 2017 in San Antonio, Texas. In the three years that I have been skating, I have traveled across the United States to skate at events, met other skaters and learned about the different styles and history of roller skating. I am a prodigy of the JB Chicago style of roller skating. My mentors, Stanley Randle and Tony Bladez, are originally from Chicago. We met at my local skating rink. They originally taught me the fundamentals of JB skating and it has been one of the most important factors of my skate journey. Since I am not originally from Chicago, I am passionate about learning the style, moves, and culture properly while representing it the correct way with all my heart. I have always been athletic and willing to push my limits with new challenges, from playing soccer at a young age, doing extreme power tumbling for fifteen years, and playing competitive paintball for two years.

When I tried roller skating for the first time at my little sister's birthday party, I was hooked. Skating one day a week turned into three days a week. Those three days a week turned into five days a week. Over time through skating, I found my second home at the local skating rink, meeting new friends and ultimately making some of my best memories. In my first couple months of skating, I bought my first pair of skates which were Riedell 851 low tops. I continued to use those until I found out about all the different styles of skating and which style naturally came to me. On my first adult night, I met Stanley and Tony from Chicago and noticed their unique footwork.

I thought to myself, "No one else in the rink was doing this type of footwork and I was intrigued by how smooth and effortless they made it look."

After seeing them skate, I was eager learning their skating style. That's when I purchased my first pair of high-top skates called OG Riedells.

After posting a short video on social media with my new OG skates, Tony reached out to me and said, "Next time, you come to the adult night, we will put some work in!"

The following Wednesday, I grabbed my skates and went to the adult night session where Tony and Stanley started to teach me some of the fundamentals of JB. That was when I knew the JB style was for me. Practicing almost every day with a desire to get better, I progressed quickly by staying humble, learning every chance I could, and by having a friend record videos of me skating as frequently as possible. I used those videos to critique my moves/groove and compare it to other skaters I looked up to. Out of the many skaters, I admire Paul from the JB Committee. When the skate crew came to San Antonio, I was feeling more than inspired. This was my first time seeing a JB skater from out of state, which became a confirmation that I needed to travel abroad to meet other skaters with the same passion for JB.

I recorded multiple videos of Paul while skating and would study his footwork. This was the early development of my groove in JB skating. Even in the present day, I'm still inspired by Stanley, Tony, and Paul. In my opinion, there are three categories of JB skating: old school, middle school, and new school. All three categories may represent the same style of skating but each one has its own groove. The old school skaters are highly respected for their knowledge and experience on the floor, continuing their era of skating with smooth footwork and the fundamentals of JB. The middle school skaters incorporate the old school smooth footwork with some of the new school moves as well. They can learn from both generations, younger or older, and make it look amazing. The new school skaters incorporate flashy footwork with some of the fundamentals while skating at a much faster pace. Although those three categories may be different in their ways, they all represent a one-of-a-kind style, which is JB.

I would be considered a new school skater because I'm only twenty years old, but I have a heavy passion for the old school/middle school style of JB skating. I experienced all of these in person at my first skating event in Chicago, which took place in July of 2019. The name of this event was

Independence Roll 9 hosted by the Chicago skating legend, D-Breeze.

I would watch videos online about past Independent Roll events, so when I got the chance to travel there, learn from the source of JB and experience this level of skating in person, as well as skate with the skaters I originally watched in videos, I was beyond grateful and excited to soak up the experience. It was amazing to be surrounded by great skaters that helped me push myself to the next level. One of my favorite moments from IR9 was the OG/Legends roll call, when all the old school JB skaters got onto the floor and had it to themselves for about 10 minutes.

I felt a strong connection to the atmosphere and talent I was witnessing. I've never seen the whole floor with only old school skaters. Watching how they grooved and skated was a priceless lesson for me. The experience was so fun that when I came back to my local rink here in Texas, I was already planning another trip back to Chicago because it felt like I was meant to skate there.

Since I am not originally from Chicago but represent their style of skating, I've always criticized myself on learning the moves the correct way. After going to Chicago, I remained humble and eager to learn every chance I could. After Independence Roll 9 in Chicago, I attended multiple other events including Joi's Skat-A-Thon in Atlanta, Texas Sk8 Fair Classic in Dallas, Houston Rolling Roundup in Houston, and my second JiveBiscuit event back in Atlanta.

At each of these events, I met new skaters and made new memories that will last forever. I post videos on social media to show what I'm learning and have met many skaters through those platforms, especially JB skaters. At my most recent JiveBiscuit event in February of 2020 before the pandemic, I skated and learned from many of the people I met through social media as well as groups I had already skated with in Chicago. Those skaters and groups include the legendary JB Elite crew, JBXperience, ThaOtherGuyz, JBCommittee, The Skywalkers, JB Rebels, JB Legacy, The 76ers, the legend Push from Atlanta, SkateFiend, Hydeboys, and more. I made some amazing memories and friends during that event, but little did I know that would be the last event for some time. In March of 2020, when coronavirus hit the United States and started to spread, almost every skating event was canceled until further notice. I had to cancel hotel reservations and plane tickets for the upcoming events I was planning on attending, but despite this bad news I wanted to make the best out of quarantine.

I skated in my driveway and garage to keep spirits high during these tough times until my local rink reopened. After a while, my local rink eventually opened again but unfortunately, I still could not travel out of state due to how fast the coronavirus was spreading. After a few months went by, Kelvin Holtzclaw aka "Pooh" from the legendary Chicago skate group JB Elite came to San Antonio, Texas to give a class on JB fundamentals and the history of JB. Since I had not traveled out of state to skate since the beginning of February of 2020, I was beyond excited to have skate family from Chicago coming to Texas.

When Pooh came to San Antonio not only was I excited to see and skate with him again but to have a familiar face from out of town that skates the same style as me, was awesome. After skating the first few days with Pooh here in San Antonio and learning multiple new routines that he showed me, we got to do our showcase skate where it was just Pooh and me on the floor for about six minutes doing routines and skating together. That is easily one of my favorite moments in skating since Independence Roll 9. There are so many skaters I look up to but Pooh and the others in JB Elite crew continue to inspire me to grow on my skate journey, and also have helped guide my groove overtime, when watching and skating with them. Anytime I see those guys, it is nothing but love on and off the skates and that is what it's all about for me.

I will always consider myself a student to the style of JB and I look forward to skating in Chicago any chance I get. That is why this chapter is called "Chicago At Heart" because that is exactly what I represent. My skating journey has only just begun but it will be exciting to see what I will accomplish over time with hard work and a straight-up passion for roller skating. I am planning multiple trips back to Chicago starting in 2021 to skate the regular sessions and learn from the local skaters there.

No matter how hectic and crazy life can get, going to the rink always helps me clear my mind and focus on what is important in my life. There is rarely a dull moment at the rink, especially if I am with a group of friends who enjoy roller skating just as much as I do. I encourage anyone reading this to give it a try and if you're already a skater… keep rolling!

King Washington

Henry Washington aka King Washington

I was born in the small town of Kinston North, Carolina. My mother, Ms. Margaret Washington, was so glad when she had me because I was a special young man. I have come a long way from my humble beginnings, and I have been blessed to travel the map.

I had a very rough childhood coming up. My stepfather was a very mean man, who would beat me, my mother, brother, and sister. I can remember very vividly how he used to hit my mother.

One day when he was hitting on my mama, I balled up my fist.

He said, "Boy if you ball your fist up again, I'm gonna shoot you." And he put a pistol at the crack of my backside.

I was so pissed, but again, when he was hitting on my mama, I balled up my fist, he ran after me with a shovel, trying to hit me. This type of abuse went on for a while.

When I was thirteen, I ran away from home. I came back when I was seventeen years old. But when I came back, I had a thirty-eight pistol on my side. I told him if you hit my mother, brother or sister again, I will shoot you. God was good because I never had to use the gun. My mother never allowed us to get rid of him. My mother was a great woman – God bless her soul.

I was introduced to skating by a friend of mine, who asked if I wanted to go roller skating.

I didn't know what it was, but I said, "Yes, sure."

We went to the rink in Kinston and I felt so free on the skates. I started doing things that night that could have broken my neck. It felt as if I was born to skate. My mother always said I was special. While she loved my brother and sister, of course, I was secretly her favorite.

I have been skating ever since that day. I love skating. I love making people happy, making them laugh. I enjoy it when we all come together and enjoy each other. Me, my cousin, and friends used to walk from New Bern North Carolina to Kinston, which is thirty-seven and a half miles, to go skating. We would just walk, talk and enjoy each other's company so the walk didn't seem so long. When we got to the rink, yes, we were tired, but we still skated, all night. My cousins, Davie Lee, Dookie Boy, Donna, Tony, Tim, and I made this trip more times than I can remember. We would always catch a ride back, which was a blessing because it was pitch dark down those dirt roads. This was how I got my name "Skate King". They said that I was the best in the bunch, not to brag but I was the best. I later joined a group called the East Coast Skaters. Boy! Was this group amazing?

I later moved to Laurel, Maryland with a family friend to work in her home, babysitting her small children. I started to skate at Seabrook and Skate Palace and attended local skate parties. It felt like I was living a great life. There in Laurel, I joined a group called Baltimore Coast Rollers and later joined Red Hot & Rollers, a predominantly white group. They loved my style and skill and used to pay me to skate. The Red Hot & Rollers made me feel like I was a star. They would pay me one thousand dollars a show, and I felt like I was rich.

I later learned they were paying me way less than they paid the white members. I didn't show up to one event after finding out. The team mother (manager) came looking for me when I refused to show up for that performance and asked me why I didn't want to skate. I told her they weren't paying me like the white members. After that show, she made sure I was paid one thousand six hundred dollars, like the others. People tended to take advantage of me because they knew I loved to skate and didn't care about the money.

I later joined the Anacostia Rollers and friends in DC. Then, I got tired of groups and decided to skate solo. This was the best decision of my life.

I shared my skate life with my mom. Yes, my mother was a skater. One time, my mom, my sister (Betty Jean), and I skated in a play called Mr. Big in Anacostia Park in DC. If you know the song and have seen the video, then you will understand the storyline, where my mom and sister Betty Jean fought over me to see who I would go with. Of course, I chose my mother. This play was such a hit and we enjoyed being part of the cast. My mother received a plaque for being the best acting queen for her performance. That's my mom and I love her so much. She passed away on November 22, 2010. I truly miss her.

There was a time I sprained my ankle and broke my little toe. The doctor put a hard cast on my leg so I couldn't skate. I love skating so much that I went to the rink that night. I sat at the rink, wondering how I could skate with this cast on. After a few moments of thought, I went into the bathroom. I put my foot in the sink, soaked my cast part of the way off, then pulled out my pocket knife and cut the remainder of it off. I put on my skates and didn't feel any pain once my foot got into those skates. I had the greatest time that night. I felt like I was skating on air.

Being at the rink brings me a feeling of joy. It's a place where I don't have to worry about fighting or discord. When I go to the rink, it has a family feeling. Skating is a stress reliever for me. There was a time I attended the Skat-a-thon in Atlanta Georgia for a Harlem themed party. I was dressed in an orange zoot suit and was skating so hard. I did a couple of tricks before I fell and broke my rib.

My friend said, "Man you need to go to the emergency room."

I said, "Nope, take me to CVS."

We went to CVS, where I got some bandage and tape, and found a cardboard box. I taped myself up and went back to the rink to continue skating for the remaining part of the night. I still have a bump on my side where the rib never healed correctly.

My advice for the younger generation is that skating is a great thing, it keeps you out of trouble, and off the streets. It's a great exercise and you get to meet a variety of different people.

Monday, at our rink, is gospel night. It is a great thing to see so many kids come out to the rink to listen to gospel music and skate. It is a way to bring the people closer to one another. My mother was my inspiration. She always encouraged me to continue roller skating and do what I do best. I generally attend twenty to twenty-five national skate events per year. This brings me happiness.

My advice to the younger generation, don't take a wooden nickel from anyone and do not try to be someone you are not. I am and will always be the Skate King or as I am referred to now as "King Washington".

If I died today, I would be happy. I love my kids, family, and friends. I am happy now and will always be. God has got my back and I believe in Him.

Cpa/Money Man/Skater

Chuck Burch aka Chuck from Detroit

I was born and raised in Detroit, Michigan, in a single-parent home as the oldest of three children. Neither of my parents completed college and my father left when I was a child. My mother demanded that my siblings and I be good students, encouraged us to excel academically and engage in athletics. She kept us busy so that we would avoid getting caught up in the perils of Detroit streets. She modeled an exquisite work ethic while providing love and support every day. We didn't notice what we didn't have. We had love. We were around like-minded people, going through the same experiences. That was enough for us to get by.

Though my mother and father met while roller skating, it wasn't until I was in my college years at the HBCU, North Carolina A&T, that I rediscovered Roller Skating in a big way. My friends and I started sponsoring roller skating parties on campus. We developed a reputation for throwing some of the best parties in the city for years.

After graduation, I moved to Houston, Texas, and rolled onto the skate scene. A few years later, I relocated to Dallas, Texas. I kept right on rolling and now I am titled as an OG in the skate world. Today, I use roller skating as physical and mental therapy. I also use it as a method to raise scholarships for students.

I find time to give back to the community in meaningful ways. I started with a golf tournament between a few friends then expanded to other interests and a nationwide scholarship fund. I realized that with just a golf tournament and a roller skating party, I could raise between Ten to Fifteen thousand dollars a year as a 501(c)(3) non-profit organization! Today, we have raised and awarded over one hundred twenty-five thousand dollars in scholarship awards since we started twenty years ago. It's a blessing to be a part of that. My advice is to find a way to tap into networks of support that uplift you and give back if you can. Not only will it be personally meaningful, but it may open the door to future opportunities and increase your level of success.

My Incredible Skatelove

Lynna Davis aka Lynna Moving Star

Roller Skating has been extremely essential in my life, mentally, physically, spiritually, and financially. It all started in Detroit, Michigan. Being a native Detroiter, roller skating was a prime example of fun, exercise, entertainment, and creativity. It was taboo for us to go to the roller rinks due to the fear that Mom and Dad had for our safety.

"Ma, can we go roller skating at the Arcadia?"

"No," was her answer. "How many times do I need to tell you? They have fought and sometimes people get killed. No, you're not going and don't ask me that question again. Find something else to do."

Well, little did she know that we were sneaking off to the Arcadia Roller Rink. My brother and I would go and be amazed by the skills of the skaters. Most times, we would just stand at the rail and feel the breeze from the locomotive speed of the skaters. We were in absolute awe just watching. When I finally got the nerve to get on the skate floor, blood rushed through my body. I knew that once I became a defensive skater instead of an offensive skater, I would be good.

In the mid-1980s, I moved to New York City to pursue a career in show business. Not only did I study acting and multiple kinds of dancing, I made sure I found time for roller skating.

During this time, no real roller rinks existed in Manhattan. We had small clubs. I remember the Village Skate and Metropales. We had several rinks in Jersey, Laces and many other rinks. I was skating four, maybe five, nights a week. We had a rink in the Bronx named Skate Key. Oh! We turned it out every time we went.

When the Roxy Roller Rink opened, I became an official without a membership. Every Wednesday, my friends and family knew exactly where I was, Lynna' was at the roller rink. Sometimes, friends would ask if they could go with me.

I would say, "Of course but once I get there, you are on your own because I'll be busy skating. Yes, I'll take you around a few times, but this is my skate night. It's my me time. Time to use my body to its fullest extent. I have to go in to release any stress I might have. Try new things on my wheels. Skate around the rink as many times as I could. Warm my body up."

As soon as I was there, then I knew it was time to go to the middle of the rink and show out and dance on my skates like it was the last party on earth.

Then, I would say, "Oh, please! Please! Play one of my favorite songs. Yeah, the one by James DTrain. Keep on."

The chorus is, "The sky is the limit. So, we just have to keep on keeping on."

I loved hearing Patty Labelle's 'The Rhythm in My Soul'. There's a line in that song she sang, "I can dance upon a dime, give back five cents, keeping time. The one thing you can't take from me is the rhythm I feel deep in my soul."

When daylight came, I was leaving the dance/skate floor. By nighttime, I was back for more. Oh, yes! When the music comes on, skaters get into a zone that only they know about.

Skaters would come up to me and say, "Do that again."

I would reply, "What did I do?"

I was so caught up in my skate zone that I didn't always know what I had done. Oh, skating can make you feel so good. You really don't want to stop. The vibe in the skate circles is the most incredible. Sometimes, it depends on what a person is there for.

I wasn't into dating where I skated. I've seen how it caused many problems and could ruin what you came to do. Then, on the flip side, some people found their spouses there. Many of us came to do the same thing:

skate and create.

Everyone having a rocking roll jamming good time.

While skating at the Roxy Roller Rink, I was with the Emperor Clothing Designer, Ellie Tahari, the Magnificent Bill Jamming Butler, Actor Khalil, and a host of Celebrities. My skating skills took me to Japan to open for a brand, 'Peace, Love, and Happiness', a fashion show in Mexico. It allowed me to perform the 'Half-time show of the New York Knicks, Trolls Movie Promo Choreographer, and Casting. Avicii made me official, they gave me the title of Choreographed Casting Director & Consultant. My skating skills also took me to Abc Localish Casting; The Big Celebrity Fundraiser Robinhood Foundation, Casting thirty Skaters; Cynthia Rowley Fashion week, casting twenty skaters; Targets XXO ANNIVERSARY, the launch of a Corporate Celebrity Designer party, Former Ladies of Chic Skating trio, NYC Roadrunners skate show at the finish line, Featured Skater Show Lost in the Disco.

Skate to Fame Venue
Here are a series of classes that get you ready for Showtime Music Videos Stage shows Film & TV.

When you find your passion, God will make sure you get paid.

SKATE 2 FAME
Helpful Hints
Skating is not a competition, it's an expression of skills, style, and creativity.

If a skater or anyone ever tells you to stay in your lane, just say, "That's Lame. God blessed me not only with the highway, I'm also blessed with the skyway. Amen. God has blessed us all with many talents. In my house, there are many mansions. If not, I wouldn't have told you so."

Never take credit from another skater and try to make it yours. Just because you change the music or eliminate other talent does not make it your property, just for social media fame. *NOT GOOD.*

Most successful people work hard to get where they are. I know it may look like an overnight success. No, it takes many hours, days, and years to arrive there.

Be sincere about what you want from another person. This will allow you to have a wonderful relationship with yourself and others.

Most times, it is not just about your talent. It's also about your integrity and honesty. Respect for others and self-respect will take you a long way. Amen ❖❖❖❣

Atlanta Passing The Skate Torch

Tony Sailor aka Sick on Skates

To break down the ATL Skate Style, you must understand the history of Atlanta Culture. The language, attire, music, and beliefs all affect how we skate. Think of a family of seven, mother and father, who married and produced five children. Understand that the style was created because of the black household. Therefore, the moves are related in some form or fashion, sharing unique sequences and swag. Those interested in learning the style must trust the process.

The Style can be described by visualizing aggressive but coordinated movements, which mirror the cadence of a song. These are created in forms of a drum major, step master, or choir. When you bring the same to skates, you will discover that movements, mostly, are done in unison. If you're raised in the South, you can identify with the musical tunes that rattle the streets of Atlanta- gospel or hip hop.

This gives birth to certain iconic dances that originated and evolved from this region. The move called "The Skate" is still in practice and taught on and off skates. It has become universal to each era in Atlanta. It is demonstrated in the skating routine called "The Stab". It was a normal movement in the Yeek Style of the dance routine called "The Devastator". The connection between skating and dancing goes hand-in-hand in Atlanta. Music can alter how we feel and, when combined with skating and dancing, it comes out to express what is being played. For it to make the list under ATL style, however, it must fall under certain criteria to be acknowledged. That is another subject for a different occasion.

Social media has played a role in delivering our content by influencing others to create something similar. Skating evolves as we grow in life. It's fun and entertaining at the same time. Many of us stay connected because of this activity we share, which becomes even more interesting when we can showcase our skills to one another. We relied on one another and focused on learning as much as possible. We couldn't force our skills and talent. We could only do what was normal at the time: trust the process.

The more authentic the song is to the region, the better it is to understand the expression of the movement by the inhabitant of the area. Since we may have been born in different eras, the era determines the movement that would become catchy to the masses in that region. This movement would become popular and develop a name.

For example, "Seeking" or "Yeek" is a popular style developed in Atlanta that began in the early 80's. A group of individuals formed a crew called "FDC" or Fresh Dancing Crew. The style they created evolved to many movements and routines that branched out to those who could skate. Most of the known iconic dance battles and music performances took place in skating rinks. This became a tradition that was passed from generation to generation. And like any era, evolution took place.

ATL Skate style has many known forms of movement. The Stab, The Prep, Bounce, and Ryde can all be linked back to Yeeking. Sick on Skates Crew, a group of talented skaters have continually demonstrated the ATL skate style and incorporated new variations with each generation.

There have been many older individuals, who taught and mentored the style. They include Vaughn Newton, Anthony Francis, Levy Johnson, DeAngelo Holt, Breeze Goodman, Keith Donaldson, and AL Fleming "ATL Skate Man". These men are the OGs or the architects of ATL Skate Style. And throughout my life, I have been fortunate to learn from them all.

I was born and raised in Los Angeles, California. I began skating at the age of three. My parents split just before I turned five. When I visited my father in Atlanta, Georgia, the seed was planted when my father brought me to "Jellybeans". This rink is a place where the style was groomed and created. At the age of thirteen, my mother decided to return to Atlanta, and from there, skating found a place with me, yet again.

Once I turned seventeen, I was already mingling with the OGs, trying to learn and keep up. At nineteen, I became a member of skate crews at local rinks such as Golden Glide. I later formed Georgia Rampage or "GRP" skate crew in 2005. The idea behind the birth was to show others in the city and communities the essence of a co-ed local skate crew.

During the years of growing, the awareness of our style and having many successes along the way, I was called to serve my country for the second time. Thus, the team was left in the care of those I hoped understood the logic behind the crew's mindset. Unfortunately, upon my return, the crew suffered compromising issues leading to financial and toxic leadership. This situation, which led to the dismissal of members, forced me to permanently dissolve GRP INC. Nonetheless, rogue individuals persisted and continued to operate GRP, but eventually succumbed to its downfall. Luckily, the passion and desire I had for skating still existed; thus, in 2009, the creation of Sick on Skates Crew came to be.

This time, I wanted to go deeper into the history of where the ATL style originated. I removed myself from what I learned from rink peers and searched out those from that past. Throughout my search, I was joined by like-minded individuals such as Corey Bing, who helped maintain structure and balance within the crew. In 2016, SOS was able to link and connect to the founding fathers of the ATL style, who gave guidance on the origin and took the time out to teach us the basics of the style.

This allowed us to adopt the old and combine it with the new. SOS became relevant within surrounding communities and the younger generation by incorporating the style in areas that have nothing to do with skating. This effort benefited from the desire of families and friends to become involved in a growing and existing movement. The crew's efforts have also made a staple in different cities around the United States and have even touched other countries.

As we continue to learn increasingly about the history, we understand how the current generation develops their interpretation of the style. SOS is the first but has been replicated with few tweaks. SOS development has led to teaching and mentoring the youth.

In 2020, SOS produced Kidz Sick on Skate's crew, which focuses on mentoring children and families. Reconnecting the families wishing to skate with each other is a joy and gift at the same time. Skating is an activity many of us enjoy doing together. It is the cohesion that we share amongst our skate mates. Luckily for us, we can pass the torch for others to build and learn from.

Now, things are starting to make sense and, for some of us, passing the torch has been a major achievement. Things have come full circle and what we like to pass along to all interested in our style: just trust the process.

The Origin Of Sk8 Vidzz

Doug Mike aka Sk8 Vidzz

In 2009, I started back roller skating after a twenty plus year hiatus without skating. I used to attend a local session in Macon, Georgia on Saturday with my family. I would take my two daughters and my wife. We would go for a couple of hours and just enjoy ourselves. We tried to do it every Saturday. Eventually, I met some regular guys my age, who encouraged me to come to the adult session on Sunday night.

I attended the adult session and thought, "Yeah, I love this. Let's do it."

I kept attending the adult session, started doing routines, learning the routines, and having fun with them. Eventually, I got hooked on a style of skating called JB. Chicago is widely known for this style and I became fascinated by some of the moves.

We had a skater that knew this style even though he was not from Chicago. He was from Atlanta but regularly visited Chicago where he learned the style from the Chicago skaters. He brought their style to Atlanta and started skating the JB style.

I began searching for JB skating on YouTube and started learning the moves by watching the videos. Eventually, I started going to Atlanta with the guys. We planned some trips to go to Golden glide Roller Rink in Atlanta. They had a late-night session from 11:30 pm to 3 am. I was amazed and fascinated at the talent and skill level of these skaters in Atlanta. I was blown away, to say the least. They were so many different styles of skaters.

I was captivated by the genres of music that were being played, which was different from our local session in Macon.

There, I saw a couple of people skating the JB style and started recording them with my cell phone. That was the beginning of skate videos and the birth of Skate Vidzz.

Keep in mind that this was a local session in Atlanta, a weekly session on Friday nights at Golden Glide. I began searching for roller skating and roller skate videos on the internet. During my search, I learned about a skate party called Skate-a-Thon, where people skate during Labor Day weekend in Atlanta from midnight until 6:00 a.m. I guess that's why they called it skate-a-thon because it was an all-night thing.

I said, "You know what? I got to go check this skate-a-thon thing out."

I told my wife that I would like her to go to this thing called Skate-a-Thon since skaters come from around the world to Atlanta to roller-skate all night long.

She's said, "I'll go with you. I'll check it out."

When we got there, our first issue was finding a parking space. The event was at Cascade and the parking lot was cram-packed full. We had to park across the street and walk across MLK Blvd, down the hill before we got inside.

I was just blown away by how many people were there. At first, my wife was in awe and all she could do was sit down to watch it. The floor was packed with around one thousand two hundred to one thousand five hundred people on the floor at the same time.

She was a beginner skater and hadn't been going on the trips to Atlanta with me. I left her to sit and watch while I went to find my tribe. After skating for a while, I recorded all kinds of footage. It was just the beginning of a beautiful relationship with me, skating, and capturing the elite skaters around from around the world that came to Atlanta to display their skills.

They did the roll call that night. I had never seen a roll call in person. I was just in a euphoric state of awe. This was the beginning of my skating journey in capturing skaters on film in their essence.

Little did I know, at the time, that it was the birth of Skate Vidzz. I hadn't started the Facebook page, but was just reaching out to skaters and befriending them. Whenever I saw 'skate' on people's profile and felt they were skaters, I would send a friend request.

I know they were thinking, "Who's this guy from Macon, Georgia sending me this friend request."

They didn't know me from Adam but in time, they learned about the name Doug Mike.

Eventually, I lost my Skate Vidzz page on Facebook. Back then, I was happy whenever I got 50 views whenever I posted a video of a skater. I started recording everybody just so I could get to know people on an individual basis, and they would get to know who I was. They say one person can't change the world, but I knew that if I could touch each individual or capture them on their skates, eventually, they would get to know me and my brand. That was the beginning and the launch of Skate Vidzz in 2014.

When I was able to get back on Facebook, I wanted to show people like myself, who didn't know about the underground culture of roller skating that people still enjoyed roller skating.

Roller skating is a passion and hobby of many. People spend thousands of dollars on roller skating equipment, roller skate wheels, outfits travel hotels, and airplane tickets - just to go roller skating and that's what I want to expose others to.

Everybody has a hobby. There are people who golf and spend thousands of dollars on their equipment. Think of any hobby that people spend a lot to get their equipment, roller skating is no different. Now, you can invest into your craft when you are ready to sacrifice your time and effort to learn different moves, styles of skating, and different routines etc. You also have to invest in the other things that go along with it if you want to elevate yourself.

You don't have to; you can just go to your local session if that's what you want to do and there are plenty of people that do it, who have never traveled outside of their local area or their regular home rink, especially some of the older skaters.

That's why I started going, not just to the skate parties but going to local sessions, hitting the local rink, and capturing the local skaters in their essence. Fast forward to 2021, as I look back at my journey of traveling as a skate videographer around the country, I can honestly say that I've pioneered and birthed a whole generation of videographers. I was the first one to bring out a gimble on the skate floor. I was the first one that launched a drone at the skating rink at a National skate party. And I can honestly say that I don't mind handing the torch down to the next generation of videographers. I played my part and did it with love because it was a passion, and I didn't do it seeking any monetary value.

I never really got compensated for my time and my efforts of traveling and capturing these skaters. When I launched my merchandise line back in 2019 I started it to get compensated for my time and effort. Honestly, I wouldn't change a thing if I looked back at my journey because it was this journey that built me into the person that I am today.

I'm glad that I could inspire the next generation. Shoutout to the next generation of videographers like Chad Ha of Skate Lyfe TV, Malik in Chicago of Chicago JB Skate.

Every time I go to an event, I meet different videographers from around the country. They might not know my face, but they've heard of Skate Vidzz and they pay homage to the work that I put in every day.

For the last five years, I posted a skate video each day. I did this out of love, joy, and passion for our culture as well as to give exposure to our culture. It wasn't for one person and wasn't for me because roller skating is bigger than me. It's bigger than any one individual, any group or any style or any city.

Roller Skating is worldwide, and I post videos so others can get a taste of the enjoyment that roller skating brings to people. It's one of the best exercises you can do. It's a wholesome family activity or one you can do by yourself. You can just go outside your house and skate on the sidewalks, your driveway, or skate at the park. You'll still get that same feeling of euphoria rolling on eight wheels. So, long live roller skating along with the roller skating community.

Skate Vidzz out!!

A Time To Sk8

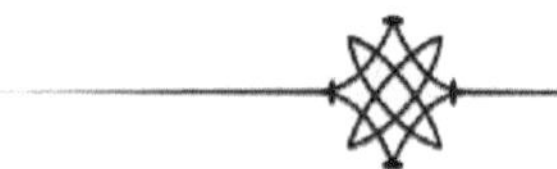

Leonard Butler aka Skate King

My name is Leonard Butler, aka Skate King. I call myself King. It's not my name. It's actually my nature. I've been skating now for four years and it's been awesome. It's been an amazing experience. I'm still learning the culture and artistry; I consider myself a novice, a newbie if you will. I skated as a youth back in Florida. I'm a Florida native.

Yes, we skated as youths from eight years old to around twelve years old. You know when you get to twelve, you get a little grown. I didn't feel that skating was cool anymore. However, the things that I do know now in terms of roller skating abilities are incomparable to what I did then. As kids, we were having fun and socializing, but when we came to Houston, I just fell in love with skating all over again. I saw some things and thought, "Woah, this is phenomenal."

What truly ignited my desire to skate was, the heartbreak of divorce. I needed an outlet, a positive outlet. I never drank, smoke, or frequented clubs. I was looking for a place to marry my passions. I love to dance and I love music.

I needed a place to marry those two. This led me to start skating with my then six-year-old son. We would go to the rink located in Katy, Texas and we would skate together. After a while, I bought some old rink dink skates, which helped me feel my way around. At this rink, you get to see all the traffic, the little people. That's what brought me back to skating. It was an outlet for me. I was skating about four times a week. I would find any open rink in Houston and hang out there. At that time, Almeda Roller Rink was popular, but to my dismay, it was only going to be open for another two months. But while there, I caught the passion, the fire, and that's what opened up my skate world.

I thought to myself, "Woah, this is ridiculous, in a good way."

You know the things I saw people doing was crazy (the moves, the vibes, the energy) and inspiring.

While I love music and dance, I quickly learned that skating is a different genre. It's a different breed. There are certain moves and pivots and things that you really have to understand, which must be stored in your muscle memory. I think the main thing is having courage and it took a lot of courage. Thankfully, some of the guys I skated with were around my age. Now, I'm not even ashamed of my age, I'm thankful. I'm fifty-two years old and started skating at forty-eight.

A lot of guys were like, "Man I used to do this and used to do that."

As for me, I was so naïve but athletic as well. I liked challenging myself and pushing myself. Again, for me, it was a positive outlet, something I could do on a regular to get rid of my stress.

When I hit the rink, boom, I'm in a sanctuary, the music playing, and it's all good.

A style of skating that I love is the New York style. It's classy, intriguing, and takes a specific skill set. You've got to be very disciplined to skate the New York style of skate. It's kind of wild, where you're moving and moody. Some other methods might just be like a flash, but the New York style is real conservative. It's like a grown and sexy kind of skate. It's New York style for me, and then I like to incorporate other little moves in there because of I'm kind of ambidextrous that way.

When I walk in the rink, my mind clicks. I love fashion, dance, and music. For me, a combination of those three worlds come together at one time and I'm feeling a sense of being social. I say hello and greet the people that are there. I want to feel and hear the music. Most importantly, I want to put my skates on and get on the wood. I want to feel that wood under my feet.

Once my breathing becomes intensified, blood starts flowing, I feel my body loosening up, then I feel a sense of freedom, a sense of sanctuary. I go to a place where no matter what's happening in my peripheral worlds, I don't mind. In that moment, I'm on the wood. The music is good. The people are good. I'm good. I'm safe. I'm having a great time.

Allow me to digress for one second. The first thing for me even before I get to the rink, I give God thanks. He's my boss, and I thank him for the agility, for movement, and being inspired to skate.

I would call skating my therapy. Yes, it is therapy, a medicine of sorts.

Just so that you can know a little bit about me. By day, I am the CEO of the #1 Dry Clean Ice Machines and Refrigeration Company - a commercial refrigeration company. I am a commercial contractor licensed by the state of Texas. We can repair service, sell, commercial kitchen refrigeration, ice machines, walk-in coolers, and freezers. We are licensed by the State of Texas.

When I say licensed, we can work on a one-story building or a fifty-story skyscraper. That's the gist of what we do, we service some of the famous places here in Houston such as the Breakfast Klub, the Reggae Hut, the Turkey Leg Hut, and many corporate entities. If you think about it on a smaller scale, we do ice machines as big as nine by nine or as large as a thirty by sixty room.

I entered this field after previously working as a food service director for a major hotel some years ago. I had my business degree and they were working me like a Hebrew, day and night, day in, day out. They burned me out, it was two tier managerial system and they had me work for two years without any help.

Long story short, a mutual friend introduced me to a gentleman who was an ac contractor. He later became my mentor and is still my mentor. This was twenty years ago. I went to work for him and took a pay cut from one hundred thousand dollars a year to ten dollars an hour, which I called a calculated risk.

That's boss tip number one: you have to make calculated risks that are based on long term gains.

I knew that if I could learn this trade it would propel me in my distant future, but I would have to discipline myself. I took the job and went to work for him, using my skill set as a general manager to organize his warehouse. I worked diligently and was honest. He noted that.

Long story short, he came to me one day while I was working. His name is Mr. Hunters.

He said, "Leo, you can carry that tool bag for the rest of your life, or you can go to school and be a boss like me one day." He asked if I would you like to go to school.

I said, "Sure."

He came back to me the next day and said, "I paid your first-year tuition, for air conditioner and refrigeration technology. Here's the address, show up on Monday."

I would work all day for a year, go to school four nights a week, for four hours, and he paid me ten bucks an hour. The next year, he came to me with the same song, we rehearsed it and I sung it for another year. That lasted four years, he and his wonderful wife, my god-mom, Julia, paid for four years of my education, put me through school, and I graduated top of my class.

People, please take heed. When you are faced with challenging times, be the person that pursues, persists, and consistently makes it through. My point is, don't give up.

Learn and be willing to be positive in a negative situation. If you can do that, you're going to come out as a winner every time life hits you hard. Here's a deeper personal boss tip for myself. This is how I encourage myself every morning - I pray, meditate, and strategize. I'm human. I may worry a little bit, I'm not perfect. When I exit the threshold out of my home I declare to my day. I speak to my day about who I am, and I say one word, with great exclamation - "CONQUEROR!", and I say it like a conqueror.

ABOUT THE AUTHOR:

Leonard Butler is a fifty-three-year-old successful entrepreneur, CEO, avid skater, and Houston based model. He has spent the last twenty years honing his skills as a leader in his field of commercial refrigeration, and has spent time on his leisure, using the past four and a half years to polish his passion as a skater.

Recently, Leonard aka "Skate King", has found a new way to express his keen sense of style by becoming a fashion model. Over the course of the past six months, he's been observed doing test shoots with local photographers. Fortunately, he honed his sense of style and fashion for fine haberdashery as a teen working closely with his grandmother in her home-based seamstress business. His passion for modeling grew out of a desire to get into amazing physical shape by working out and skating, creating additional income, and sharing it in print. Skate King keeps busy following his dreams and passions.

His goal is to inspire men to follow their dreams, diversely, step out of their comfort zones, and live beyond their limitations.

His favorite quotes include:
"If it doesn't fit, don't force it."
"It's the etcetera that costs you...etc... etc... etc."
"Be a gentleman at all times."

Facebook: Skate King
Instagram: @beardednlidded

To view videos of the author, grab the physical copy for an interactive experience.

Skating In The Motherland

Okurut George aka B Boy Skater George

My journey as a skater started in 2012, when I bought the skate shoe, known as rollerblades from a friend who was selling them for ten dollars.

After buying the rollerblades, I had to teach myself because I didn't have anybody to teach me. My sister never wanted me to learn skating because skaters had a bad image in the country (they were mostly known as thieves). I still wanted to learn. I had been in love and was passionate about skating.

We have bad roads in Uganda, especially in the villages. I always had to hold on to the back of a motorcycle, which would pull me through.

Skating was also something new in Northern Uganda. I remember in 2013, when I went with my skating board to school, all my schoolmates and the villagers would follow me. The Principal had to seize my skateboard because he wanted me to concentrate on studies. He told me I would get it back in 2014 after the final exams. I felt so bad, but I had to obey the rules of the school.

When I was done with school, I went to the city, where I bought new rollerblades. Then, I joined the Uganda Rollball team because I was so passionate about skating seriously and wanted to be someone great, who can inspire and motivate the young generation.

From there, I joined Supersonic Skating Academy, which had programs that taught skating at International School. I worked with them for few months to make money, but I had to go back to into construction, which was my profession.

I really wanted to get serious about skating. I faced several challenges.

Skating equipment and shipping was expensive. I couldn't afford to pay for any of those with my meager salary. Yet, I couldn't get my mind off of skating. I skated for fun but couldn't go all in because we didn't have any good skating parks.

The government doesn't support skating, even though we have a sports council in our country. They don't care about skating, which has discouraged a lot of people from skating. I would love to continue, but I will need more support in building skate parks in different regions of the country. I would love to be a genuine supplier of skating equipment because that's another big challenge.

For now, I'm teaching yoga and acroyoga to different communities because I'm certified to that. I see skating as a way to bring progress in this country. I am looking forward to overcoming the numerous challenges in front of us. With the equipment I will be able to teach more communities.

At this point, I believe that if we, as skaters around the world, come out to support one another, then we shall have a great community of skaters with a great supporting platform for the young generation in different countries.

I am excited about us coming together to make skating great in more African countries.

Thanks.

Rolling Beyond The Wood

Antwan McDaniels aka Flyy and FrreShh

May I say, "Greetings to everyone - from your very own McDaniel B FrreShh, also known in the deeply loved skate world as Sir. FrreShh."

I come to you straight from the heart and with love, but I must let you know that "I'm in love and married to my eights until the day I die and the wood is our best friend. I guess it's safe for me to say that I was blessed to have many different talents growing up. You can say I'm just an "all-round entertainer."

Skate magic did not just happen for me all of a sudden. I have been skating since the time I was a year and ten months old. Skating was popular and most of the time it ran in the family. It did for me. Mom, dad, sisters, brothers, aunties, uncles, grandma's, grandpa's: everyone did it. It was just the thing to do.

If it was your birthday, Christmas, or other holiday, if you didn't get a skateboard, then it was roller skates. It was just "the gift to give and the one that you could never go wrong with."

You were a lucky young boy if you got a bike because that was like a Mercedes for a young guy like me back in the day. It was a cool thing because you could ride around with all your friends, ride to the corner store, and maybe even give your little girlfriend or crush a ride.

I grew up as a kid loving to skate and playing little league sports as a hobby. I also liked aggressive inline skating and played high school sports while coming up as a teen. Singing R&B music, and hip hop dancing (better known as "Clown Dancing" to other natives from South Central Los Angeles like myself) was my true love.

People may see me all over the country today, but the beautiful city of Los Angeles is where I am from. It's where I grew up and where I went to school from elementary all the way through college. I was so blessed to have many different talents and skating was just another fun hobby for me when I was a young kid growing up.

It all started in August of 1989, when my parents gave my older sister her thirteenth birthday party at the "World Famous Midtown World on Wheels". It wasn't until my sister and a few other family members took their skates off to go dance near the concession area that this little baby boy felt it was the perfect opportunity to stick his little baby feet into those abandoned skates, which those "dancing" family members left behind.

One chance was all that the little baby needed because, after that, he never stopped. That little baby turned out to be Sir FrreShh. Having multiple outlets and different talents to turn to was a true blessing, especially for a young kid like me that had to grow up knowing "how to survive in South Central." Dash dancing was the real passion because my love for singing began to die down at this point. Roller skating did not become a passion for me until two extremely devastating moments happened in my life.

When I was fifteen years old, myself and many others that share the same passion for hip hop dancing, like we do in today's times with skating, we were out Clown Dancing our lives away in Inglewood at the Historical Great Western Forum. We were trying to make some amazing history for our city, our dance groups, and for ourselves as well. It was within our inner city culture of hip hop dancing, which was created by "Tommy the Clown" in the very beginning of the 1990s. I am sure that you're pretty aware of all the fun and beautiful things that Southern California, Los Angeles has to offer, which I call "The Beauty."

I'm also very confident that you know a little bit about its past crime rate, its extreme violence, and crazy gang culture. Well, at least that goes for the "South Central" part of LA, which is where I happen to be from. This also applies a to a couple of neighboring cities - like Compton, and Long Beach. If you're not aware of any of this part of LAs' history, some small examples to help give you a better idea would be movies like "Colors, Menace to Society, or even Boyz N the Hood. Very much unlike the beauty of the city, I call this part "The Beast." It's my way of painting a perfect picture of a large city like Los Angeles, which I feel has exactly that "the Beauty and the Beast."

Southern California is definitely a place of many people's dreams, but if you were one of the unfortunate young boys or girls coming up on the other side of the beauty like me and many others, then it was more like a "concrete Vietnam jungle". We had to learn how to survive in South Central. It's for sure a toughness builder, because even if you were not gang affiliated, you were still subject to falling victim to the city's abusive and bizarre warzone, where you could lose your life at any second.

Having to live under these circumstances was like having to walk on needles with a gun to your head every single day. Playing a sport, having a hobby or passion was almost mandatory to make it out alive in South LA. People all over the city and neighboring cities had clown dancing. It was our getaway, stress reliever, antidepressant, suicide prevention line, and our way of staying away from gang related consequences.

In the early 2000s, a few gang members started joining the clown dancing trend. All of us original clown dancers were starting to worry and have a level of discomfort, because we knew how these gang-related dancers would react if something had not gone their way. And sure enough, they did just that. On the night of Battle Zone Three at the Great Western Forum in Inglewood.

After a victorious night, me and my dearest brother-like friend that I grew up with were now leaving the place, the Famous Great Western Forum in Inglewood.

As we were leaving to go home, the worst thing that you could think of began to happen, the sound of gunshots rang out. We all started running in different directions and ducking on the ground until the gunshots stopped. Now that all the gunshots had stopped, of course I began to look around for my friend, only to find out that he had been shot in the head by the crossfire of a bullet. The gun had been fired by none other than those cowardly gang members that were shooting at some other dancers following a confrontation by them for losing their battle on that night.

It was horrifying, one of the worst days of my life. I couldn't believe it. That devastating event brought clown dancing to an end in my life. I was just not interested in continuing to clown dance and go on without my beloved brother and close friend. I retired from clown dancing completely.

As life went on for me, I rolled on with a broken heart, but a more fiery and passionate purpose. I carried all my passion for dancing into roller skating. Everything that I had done when I was dancing followed me, including my shoes, clothing, colors, socks, and skate laces. Skating became my new fashion.

Now in my teens, I was really starting to evolve as a dancing skater that was known to wear a lot of exciting colors as if I was still clown dancing to this day. Little did they know how much everything, which they could see at their eyesight was personally connected to me in real life away from the skating rink.

Fast forward to a couple of years later, I was seventeen years old and getting ready to walk the stage in high school, I was already rolling with the punches. Life threw what I considered to be its most unexpected and devastating blow at me.

One sunny bright Saturday morning in Southern California, I was around the corner at my friend's house, shooting some early hoops. As I was enjoying the moment, my other neighbor and friend came running to me from around the corner of my house, to tell me the worst thing that I think you can tell anyone. He came to tell me that he had gotten the news that my mom had passed away in a car accident. Because it was so sunny, bright, and beautiful outside I didn't believe him.

I opted for knowing the truth and did the only thing I could. In a split second, I dropped the basketball and sprinted back around the corner to my house to see if the horrific news was true. I found out that the life-changing news was no fairytale. The sunny and beautiful Saturday morning turned out to be the most devastating, heartbreaking, darkest, life crushing, and horrifying day that life could ever bring me.

It was January of 2005, I was seventeen years old at the time getting ready to graduate, and my mom passed without getting her ultimate reward of seeing me walk the stage. My entire world was totally shattered. Right at that point, I didn't know if this horrific life situation was going to make me abandon skating, or if it would bring me closer to it. Honestly, I really didn't give a damn at that specific moment in my life. My whole life was just DARK. I didn't even care to graduate, but I knew that my mom would want me to walk that stage and go on to make her proud. It was an extremely trying time for me that year, and the years that followed. Already with a shattered heart, I was still healing, but life delivered more devastating blows to me.

I experienced the loss of six family members within two years. It was so terrifying that I thought I was going to be the next one to die. I was so grateful that God gave me the courage and faith to take on all and any of life devastating blows, and for me to keep on keeping on. I mustered up enough courage, not only to fight all the adversity life was putting me through while totally drowning my hope and passion for roller skating, but to be able to stand tall and proud to say I still walked that stage with everything going on. I know that I made my mother proud.

It was an extreme blessing to have a drug like passion to turn to called roller skating. After the loss of my mom, my passion for skating had taken off to a whole new height. When I graduated, it was a tremendous accomplishment because I was the first male in my generation of the family, along with one other cousin, to cross that stage. Despite me being on the honor roll, graduating with straight A's, being a star player on the football, basketball, volleyball, softball, tennis, soccer, and the track team, it didn't seem like it was enough.

I even graduated as a Cadet Lieutenant Colonel out of the JROTC program, earned an Art scholarship to the amazing University of Southern California, and earned a scholarship to go to the College ROTC Program at Texas A&M.

Sadly, none of those amazing accolades were enough for me to earn a little support from the family members that were still alive. *Heartbreaking right?* My older sister was hurting from the loss of our mother too and could only do what she could do. The Honorable McDaniel B FrreShh still ended up sleeping on Skid Row, with rats running by him, like it was all so normal before finally receiving a helping hand. Before this point roller skating was the only thing there for me. I then knew because it was all so clear what roller skating meant to me and my life, and how important it was for me to do it.

I'm someone who doesn't drink or smoke, and never have. I've always got my high from one of my God given talents. But I was no longer really doing any of them after graduating from high school, except for football. I didn't have the necessary support system, so my burning passion and devoted love for skating had beat everything else out at this point.

There was nothing better for me to do other than get my roll on. I'm extremely proud to say that I'm in a skate love relationship. I have now come to find out that skating is the full package, where I am able to express the emotions of all my different talents. (It's my tequila shot, and my Mary Jane, all in one, except that allows me to get high spiritually and physically as well. Just a total win-win).

I don't care what age group you were in. If you were a roller skater and grew up in LA on the west coast, or anywhere as a matter of fact, if you were a breathing human being, the original Midtown World On Wheels was the place to be. This place always offered a loving and home feeling kind of environment to those who truly came to skate, was looking for fun, and to create a ton of amazing memories.

World on Wheels was LAs' only inner-city rink after all the many other nearby rinks had been shut down due to violence, or gentrification over the years. It was known for being the most poppin place in the city, once upon a time, and was the only major place that guaranteed to give you the time of your life.

Now that you know I've been a victim of all those horrifying things from the beginning until now, it should be easy to see why and how skating went from being my hobby and just a regular love, to a fiery burning passion, and mandatory thing in my life. For me and tons of other LA Natives, roller skating played a critical part in surviving South Central. If you look closely, you'll find the quote 'skate or die' on a lot of my skates and their tires. Roller skating is my only go-to. It's where the people that I call family are at, and I'm sure there are many skaters that can relate.

Anyway, the World Famous Original Mid-Town World on Wheels was everything to sacrifice for. It helped deal with inner-city living conditions, brought joy, was a total breath of fresh air and saved the lives of many youth.

From the time I left home until the moment I arrived, I felt pure excitement. It was even more exciting getting out the car, walking towards the rink, down those stairs, or up the stairs, or directly in, like at any other rink. Having to stand in line on the ramp, or to go down those stairs at World on Wheels to get to the line in the lobby, right before it was time to be let in to go skating, was an experience of its own.

I would just look around to see and feel everyone's level of peace that existed, due to the overwhelming amount of love, joy, and extreme fun that I knew I was about to experience. Just like skating was the thing to do back in the day, the Original Midtown World on Wheels was the place to be. A perfect word to describe it would be family reunion because that's what it was like every time I went.

They would turn the center circle part of the skating rink floor into a dance floor for all those, who preferred to dance instead of skate at midnight. We got to dance to all the hottest Hip Hop, Reggae, and R&B music of the 1990s through the early 2000s. And let me tell you, when that clock hit midnight, it turned into Boogie Nights down there in the center circle of the rink, which was perfect for me because if you remember, before skating turned into a mandatory thing in my life, singing and dancing were my original first love. Having the option to get out there and dance or skate my life away, was something for me to live for.

The 7 pm to 7 am parties that took place once a month would attract quadruple the amount in people than a regular skate session. I mean the whole rink was filled to capacity. Then, they would have to start turning people away. Everyone would come out; it was the perfect all-night party of a teens dream. Not to mention that the wings and fries at World on Wheels were always off the chain. The food was just one of the Great Danes that they were known for.

This place was an important staple for us inner-city people. I can't say enough how many lives were touched and saved by it, and how much more it did than just serve the community as a roller skating rink. It even played a part in some up-coming artist lives like da Brat, DJ Quik, and Snoop Dogg, just to name a few – which are now legendary. Up-coming artist performed here when they were not yet big enough to reserve a regular sized concert venue. World on Wheels always cater to those coming from the bottom, and trying to make it to the top, especially the youth. They offered a small youth program called the Street Team, for which you had to get good grades to be a part of. I enjoyed my experience as a team in this program because it offered things like after school tutoring, free food, and free skating, for teens that were ages thirteen to seventeen. If you were not old enough to be able to be legally employed, you could qualify for this program.

I have never experienced, or heard of a skating rink covering so many different platforms of community service, or playing such a critical and life changing factor as the original Mid-Town World on Wheels has for LA. I'm proud to call it my home rink. I helped fight to save it as a Historical Landmark back in 2013, so that they could not tear it down.

Skating in Los Angeles at World on Wheels, I fall under the category of a freestyle skater. Being a male freestyle skater from Los Angeles is a whole different thing. It's very smooth, but yet a funky Style with a splash of flash that requires some skill, and that you are versatile. Even though to many, we're known as CALI, I must let it be known that the LA Freestyle style of skating is like none in the world known to Skaters. This is due to original LA freestyle skating, focusing on multiple things at once like that funky West Coast Bounce, which is the number one, fundamental to our style. Their style includes a lot of body movement, footwork, jumps, lips, stumps, choreography, dancing, spinning, sliding, and a touch of many other skating styles all rolled into one.

Other skaters around the country usually focus on just one style. Being an LA freestyle skater gives me the opportunity to express myself freely without any limits due to the nature of its style or its culture.

It's not something that you have to do, but I think with a certain amount of pride and passion that you have in your heart, and for your city, will for sure push you to do it. Showing some of those characteristics are nice ways to put on, or to represent for your city while on the wood.

That's a part of what representing is about. Showing some pride and passion for what we do. I feel that it is extremely important for black skaters to represent very passionately because once upon a time, blacks were not even allowed to enter the skating rink, from the time of the first roller skate being made in 1863, and the first Roller skating rink to ever open in 1864, which both happened to take place in New York, there were no blacks allowed at that time.

Skating inside the rink was something exclusive to upper-class whites. It remained that way until the mid-1900s. Sadly, like many other things in Black History, our skate ancestors had to suffer and pave the way for us.

They were beaten with batons, and lacerated, had fire thrown at them like in riots, along with many other obstacles thrown at them. These were some things that they went through just to pave the way for blacks to one day be able to roller skate inside the skating rink. They had to fight so hard for us to be able to enjoy this passion of roller skating in a rink, the way that we do today. This is why I feel it's important for us to represent, every time we get the chance, with die hard pride and fiery passion, without taking a single second of skating inside of a roller skating rink for granted.

There was too much suffering, and it was too hard of a fight by our brave skate ancestors that paved the way, for it to ever be forgotten, or go unappreciated.

Even if it's acknowledging the history of people like Ledger Smith, a man with an abundance of courage, who almost lost his life to a racist white person that tried to run him over as he roller skated a unbelievable 685 miles all the way from Chicago to Washington to join the march with Martin Luther King for the civil rights movement on August 27, 1963. It took him a jaw-dropping 10 days.

Now, that's what I call an extreme roller skater. He was hardcore; and that's how you represent. Having respect for people like him, and the nothing-short-of-amazing Debi Thomas, should not even be an option. She was the very first African American woman to make it to the winter ice skating Olympics and was also the U.S. national champion twice. This young beauty was the world champion in 1986, only eighteen years of age. She turned right back around in 1988 and earned a bronze medal in the Winter Olympics at age twenty. People like this, which are far beyond amazing should forever be remembered and respected. They play such a critical role, breaking the ice and helping pave the way for all of us African American skaters today. And for that, I am forever so humble and grateful.

All this are more than enough for me to represent with burning passion and deep pride, every time I lace up my eights. I prefer that good ole' school.

As my mom used to say, "There's no school like the old school."

And I really believe in that because the old-school is all about that funkiness, joy, peace, family reunion, love, and happiness. It's always drama free, so it's two thumbs for me because I'm definitely about being drama free. This is why many know me for saying things like, "Skate More – Talk Less."

The only time I enjoy talking about skating more than doing it, is when I'm actually teaching its rich history and culture to whomever God brings my way.

Whenever God calls me home, it's the way I want to be remembered as skater - one who loved and appreciated the art of roller skating and respected its culture like no other; one who wants nothing but the best for the culture; one who did it from the heart every single time with an enormous amount of pride and passion. All for the love of the culture.

Now, if I were to ever be blessed to get married, I'll always be cheating because I would be out making love to the wood with my eights all the time. Haha!

You know, all of us skaters have dreams, and a few of those for me would be for the older and younger generations to close the gap so that the culture would be much stronger for much longer. Another dream of mine would be for the skaters that fell off to find a way back, and for the non-inspired skaters to get inspired and skate because like our skate ancestors kept striving to pave the way for us, we must also continue to strive and represent for the love of the culture so that we can keep rolling on.

If you've been around me, you'll know that I like to say, "Make it FrreShh."

This for me means to do it with a lot of Love, to do it with passion, to express your emotion freely, and lastly to represent in a die-hard way.

I must not let you forget that I was born in the mud, but I made it out clean. This, along with all my other talent that I grew up and things that I went through along the way, is what evolved the guy that you all know so well, Sir FrreShh.

For anyone that ever wondered what it was like coming up in LA, or what being a skater in LA was like, now you all know. Being at the one and only World-Famous Original Midtown World on Wheels is your answer because that's what it was all about.

Now, as we all continue to make skating strides and roll on, I want to remind everyone to make it FrreShh. SKATE Love, Skate PASSION, SKATE or die... Sir FrreShh

Visions Of The One Wheel Roller "The Inner Life Of Leo White"

Leo White aka Quad1

I never envisioned that a gift from God could be so powerful and life changing. As a young boy growing up in Missouri roller skating was just a leisurely pastime my family enjoyed every weekend. I recall conversations with my Father, talking about the ownership of our skating rink and the visions of bringing families and people together in unity from a small concept called roller skating.

I was introduced to the sport of skating at the age of six. Our family would skate so often it became my thriving passion to become the best on the hardwood. Skating created an avenue of escapism for me, a place where I could lace up and leave all my troubles and cares of the world on the wood as I dreamt of one day being a legend in the game. As I grew older and continued to perfect my skating style, I was introduced to "Free Style" skating through the mentorship of Bryant Morris, the first person to ever take off the back truck and wheels, mastering a unique competitive style without damaging the hardwood floors. This style intrigued me so much I became a sponge, mentally and physically mastering the techniques in pursuit of creating a style of my own.

While Bryant Morris is the first mentor in a line many, it's legends such as Lisa Boyd, Harpo, Kenny, Kevin Hollywood Brown, Wayne-O, Thomas Bouie and Adrienne, and Big George (RIP), that I've taken pieces of each one to bring full circle the creation of my brand. After competing successfully in numerous competitions, I prayed for a style that would place me above the ordinary and set me apart from all that brace the hardwood.

That prayer was answered in 1997, when I was blessed with perfecting the style of "The One Wheel Roller". This unorthodox style of skating allows me to skate using only one left front outer wheel on the left skate boot and one right front inner wheel on the right skate boot. To date, there is no skater domestically or internationally capable of skating my perfected style.

The journey of the "One Wheel Roller" hasn't always been smooth sailing. To become a perfected brand, one must endure many trials, tribulations, and sacrifices that will test the very fabric of your soul. Many a night on my knees, I've prayed for wisdom, knowledge, and humility, to move me beyond situations of adversity. Early in my career, I was homeless, hungry, and working for below minimum wage in Atlanta, Georgia to maintain the basic means of survival while pursuing my dream of becoming a skating legend. You see, it takes everyday struggles and sacrifices to build the character and integrity needed to successfully create and manage a business/brand. Knowing what it feels like at the bottom of the game strengthens my inner being to stay mentally focused in my pursuits regardless of the past or present circumstances. To conquer the mental fire within, you must learn how to tame it, not become a slave to it. The public will never understand your fire if they can't visually comprehend how you've moved beyond your trials, unsinged by their very flame.

With knowledge of survival in my veins, I decided in 2001 to aggressively perfect "Leo White", the brand as a dominating presence in the skate community. I started networking my name and skating style to businesses, capturing the eyes of some very prominent organizations to secure roles in commercials, documentaries, and movies as the "The One Wheel Roller".

Becoming well known in the urban skate arena has taught me it takes more than name recognition to build a brand, and how you present yourself to a public audience can make or break the success of your business. With this understanding, I've sharpened my tools in the business and created a brand that is now nationally and internationally known in the skating circuit.

Business is not only about branding. It's about using your influence, knowledge, and connections to further strengthen the community, public outreach, policies, and education that continue the advancement of individuals young and old in their professional pursuits. I've created a business model that will give back to our communities through mentorships, workshops, educational forums, and instructional videos and platforms. Leo's Quad One Evolution International, LLC, is an organization focused on excellence in Black Business.

As the first Black-owned skate manufacturing organization we plan to break down barriers once untouchable in the sports arena. Within my business framework, I've perfected the rollout of signature skate products, and skate apparel through our trademarked "LQ1" brand. Our organization has a strong media presence. We are also leveraging our presence on social media platforms including Facebook, Instagram, and YouTube. Our skate family, and new skate members can follow and view tutorial videos and follow me across the country as I check in with other skate venues and legends throughout the United States and abroad.

In my quiet hours, I find myself extremely humbled by the magnitude of responsibility and success God has blessed me with. It's amazing how a small prayer from a young man in pursuit of a dream can create such profound beauty that can touch so many lives. I'm blessed that roller skating is not only my passion but is now the life's blood that fuels a movement.

With an appreciation for the entrepreneurial process, no job has ever been too messy or difficult to tackle. My hands-on experience assisting in the growth of many existing franchise organizations allows me to perfect my knowledge of the business industry and arms me with a fresh perspective and focus of how to integrate my passion in building a successful business blueprint that other entrepreneurs can glean from in their individual business pursuits.

This journey continues to teach me. I'm forever a student in pursuit of perfection. If I can leave anything through my legacy, I want to impart three profound things I've learned:

First, no matter what obstacles are present in your life, never allow them to deter you from focusing on your dream. We are all given gifts from God to perfect and share with others, and we must endure the trials, tribulations, and growing pains, to ultimately manifest our gifts to the world.

Second, stay grounded. Having a strong spiritual relationship is key to success. As you climb the ladder of success in pursuing your dream, there will without a doubt be people, places, and situations used to detour you from your goals. Don't allow the external noise to drown the voice in pursuit of excellence. Mental and physical focus is key and with the unconditional love of God, all things are possible.

Lastly, I will say enjoy your dream. Have fun, embrace the joy and fulfillment of knowing you are successfully living your passion. It's a beautiful thing waking up each day knowing your life isn't about showing up for a job, because now your passion is your job. A profession I will gladly show up for any and every day of the week.

I hope that the legacy of the "One Wheel Roller" will give back to the world and those fortunate enough to know the brand of "Leo White" will gleam from my presence and the impact of excellence our business represents nationally and internationally.
(chapter written by Stacey Kannon)

In Memorium

Sending peace and prayers to those in the skate world whom we have lost but who shall never be forgotten:

Anthony (Tex) Smith
Charles (The Wood) Haywood - Philly
Linda (Lady Linda) Corley - Philly
Will (Mean Will) Reed – NYC
CD Man – STL
Scott (Slo Motion) NYC
Gary (Uncle Peaks) Pete
Morris (Philly Plash) Armstrong
Puerto Rican Mike – NYC
Pops – Ohio
Lakiesha (RedBone) Jones - NC
Jarel (Mello) Joes CCP Ohio
DJ DC – Texas
Keon Nesbitt- CCP LA
Will Nesbitt -LA
Lezly Ziering – NYC Central Park
Davie (Brooksie) Allen NYC
Monique (Skate Vixen) Williams – NJ
Allen Jetter - Philly
Duvall J Stowers - Venice Beach CA
Ever Ready – Venice Beach CA

For those not mentioned, you will forever be in our hearts, prayers, and with each roll of our wheels.